BEWARE CASUAL LEADERS

BEWARE CASUAL LEADERS

LEADERSHIP MATTERS

*A practical guide to who makes
a good leader of an engaged organisation
– and why some people will never make it.*

ANDY PORTSMOUTH

Matador
9 Priory Business Park,
Wistow Road, Kibworth Beauchamp,
Leicestershire. LE8 0RX
Tel: 0116 279 2299
Email: books@troubador.co.uk
Web: www.troubador.co.uk/matador
Twitter: @matadorbooks

ISBN 978 1838590 727

British Library Cataloguing in Publication Data.
A catalogue record for this book is available from the British Library.

Printed and bound in Great Britain by 4edge Limited
Typeset in 11pt Ten Oldstyle by Troubador Publishing Ltd, Leicester, UK

Matador is an imprint of Troubador Publishing Ltd

I dedicate this book to the following:

to Tim and Guy for their enthusiasm for the project,
their encouragement and advice on its contents;

to James and John, who continue to
enrich my life each and every day;

and to Suzannah, who has been a tireless
support and unwavering in her commitment.

Thank you.

CONTENTS

PROLOGUE

"Oh yeah! Yet another book on leadership. What makes you think you have something to say? What makes you qualified to comment? Why should I listen to you?"

All fair questions. I am not an academic. I am not a researcher. I am not a psychologist. I don't claim to be a titan of industry. I am not a famous entrepreneur, like Richard Branson, nor have I been the CEO of a worldwide business, like Jack Welch. I have not sat on the main board of a PLC, or any other organisation, and I am not even the brightest or most talented person I know. In fact I am unknown by the City and to all but the few people I have worked with.

But what I do have is thirty-five years of practical experience in some of Britain's and Europe's largest businesses, from graduate entry to operating board director and strategy consultant. I have worked in a wide variety of markets, in different disciplines, in different companies with different structures and business philosophies, and within vastly different leadership teams generating diverse business cultures. I have had reasonable success in my career with reasonably successful companies and clocked up a total of eighteen years as a director in three different companies. And I have seen and experienced some of the best and also some of the worst management practices in that time.

Almost from the first day of work I was expected to lead people. And over those thirty-five years of career, I found myself leading departments of up to a hundred people, presenting regularly to several hundred employees and representing the interests of my business unit to the main board, non-executive directors, acquisition targets, analysts and major shareholders. Yet, in those thirty-five years I have had no training in what it takes to be a leader, or what sort of person I needed to be.

I am lucky enough to have worked for large companies who still invested in training at that time. I had plenty of training in competencies to fulfil my role, and much training in the mechanics of leadership: appraisals, giving critical feedback, competency-based interviews, handling difficult conversations, how to set agendas, how to run a meeting etc. But no training whatsoever on what I think is the real challenge for a successful business – what it takes for you to be a leader; who you have to be.

A few years into my career, I found myself running teams of managers. Before that I had only a couple of people to oversee and had a low profile within the organisations I worked in. Up until then I thought it was easy to be a leader as it largely depended on strong personal relationships and frequent contact with those who reported into me. However, I was already disillusioned by the way I had personally been managed and by what I saw of the leadership style of senior managers and directors.

Even at this early stage of my career I had concluded:

o **Andy Rule #1**
If something is wrong in a business culture, you never have to look far from the top – the CEO.

- **Andy Rule #2**

  Most companies are far too casual about their employees. Their managers and directors do not value them and spend little time trying to maximise their potential – they only pay lip service to any claim that people are their most important asset.

- **Andy Rule #3**

  You can have the worst job in the world, but a good boss will make it a great job.

- **Andy Rule #4**

  No company spends significant time on selecting the right people to be leaders or on developing a leadership style.

I believe leadership is critical to the success of any organisation and I still believe that the above observations are accurate and fair today. The quality of management has never been good enough and nothing has progressed in the last generation.

It was when the teams got larger – first five people, then nine, then sixty and more – that I realised that relying on strong personal relationships and frequent contact was just impractical. Like most people I know, put in that situation, I was left to develop my own style. I had already had scores of managers in two different companies but none that I looked up to as leader. And so I concentrated at the time on avoiding what I thought were the worst ways in which I had been led by my own managers!

As my career progressed I was fortunate enough to be managed by people, and to observe others, who I appreciated were good leaders – Bernard Bremer, Roz Boulstridge, Bob Jones, Tim May. And I count myself as very lucky – a number of my peers can name far fewer people they considered to have been good managers or great leaders.

Although they were not perfect (they would be the first to say that), and I was sometimes disappointed by some of their actions, they all had similar characteristics, which helped me to understand what it took to be a leader.

After thirty-five years in business, I have concluded that people-management and leadership have never been more important. The old paradigm used to be that you were good at your job so you were promoted to supervise and train others to be as good as you. Eventually you were so good at your job, you were promoted to supervise teams so large that it included people whose jobs you had never done, which were beyond your technical competence. Eventually your responsibilities meant that you were no longer "doing the do" but managing those that did – and letting go of the detail was the hardest part of the job. But at least some of those hard-won skills were still relevant and could be applied.

Technology has moved on so quickly in the last few years that the old paradigm no longer applies. No one cares that you were once great at producing overhead projector slides, twelve-month demand forecasts in metric tonnes, building new shops, or mass-market television commercials. Not in the new world of pay-per-click advertising, just-in-time fulfilment, social-media influencers, algorithm-based demand modelling, internet sales, augmented-reality shopping experiences etc. All the skills that got you noticed, successful and promoted in the first place are outmoded and surpassed. Increasingly, today's leaders have to supervise, engage and motivate people that have skills they never had themselves and therefore cannot polish. The challenge for today's leadership is how to maximise the output and potential of people who are technically more competent than them.

You would think that in this new world companies would put enormous emphasis on leadership selection and development. Some organisations do but companies never have and sadly there is little sign that they have yet to understand the opportunity. Companies just do not take leadership as seriously as they should. I hope in this book to suggest ways in which individuals can develop a more effective approach to leadership and maximise the potential of both themselves and their organisation.

Section one

BACK TO
BASICS

WHO MADE YOU LEADER?

The CEO of a large-scale and highly successful global business is preparing for an interview with a journalist.

The stakes are high. This is a highly respected journalist, working for the most reputable of all financial newspapers.

It will be a searching interview on the CEO's leadership style and the progress of the company since he took the helm. It's important to him because of the impact on his reputation and profile within the City – future opportunities for him could rely on this. And it's important for the company as it will reassure the analysts and shareholders that the company is in a safe pair of hands to guarantee future earnings growth. If all goes well the CEO should have favourable reviews and an easier time at the next AGM.

As usual the first question is a warm-up before the main part of the interview.

"So how many people work for your company?" asks the journalist.

The CEO thinks for a moment and then says, "About half of them!"

It's a funny story isn't it? And I laughed as loudly as anyone when I first heard it. More than likely it never happened and it is just a joke.

However, there is often a kernel of truth in even the funniest joke. And life is stranger than fiction.

When you analyse the story it is not so funny. Explicitly, and casually, the CEO is criticising his employees. Implicitly, he is saying that the company would be more successful if he wasn't the victim of a work-shy workforce. But he is not the victim here! It is his employees who are being impugned with no opportunity to reply to their critic. It is they who are having their reputations tarnished, not him. Moreover, he is the leader of this workforce and has several choices to change these circumstances:

o Why not replace the poor performers with new and enthusiastic talent?
o Why not just sack half the workforce if they are not required and put the savings into the bottom-line profit?
o Why not sack half the workforce, then double the salary and bonuses of the other half and reap the benefit of the immediate improvement in morale and inevitable productivity boom?

And of course his answer would be that the trick is to know which half of the workforce is working and which isn't!

Whichever way you look at it, the CEO must be a pretty poor leader to know that he has half the productivity he should have and then publicly declare it without being mindful of the impact *on all* of his employees. And it's a poor leader that blames the people who he is responsible for leading!

And while that may just be a story, and might never have happened, the following are real and did. Real life is stranger than fiction!

- ✗ -

Back in the 1990s, a CEO of one of Britain's largest companies was being interviewed by the financial press. A few years before, he had had the privilege of being selected to lead a company that was one of the most well known and trusted in the country and which had built an enviable reputation over decades in the UK and global markets.

However, the latest recession had severely impacted performance and results had disappointed the City. At the same time, it was rumoured that corporate raiders were preparing an aggressive play to take over the company, which was cash-rich at the time. The CEO had made a unilateral and particularly bold decision which was subsequently roundly criticised within the City as both a bad fit with strategy and likely to yield a poor return on investment – criticism that sadly proved to be extremely accurate! The CEO had then brought in a team of business consultants to overhaul the strategy and business processes.

In the interview the CEO was asked how he justified the length of time the consultants had been in the business and their high cost. His reply was widely reported amongst his employees as it was to the effect that *the business was sound if only he could get the idiots in his management team to make better decisions.*

The HR director of the same company was also interviewed by local radio. The recession had affected employment and large layoffs of workers were being made by many companies, across the board, in every sector and all over the country. The fear of redundancy was palpable at every layer of every workforce.

The company was one of the largest employers in the region where its head office and operating offices were based. Not only was the workforce large but many generations of the same families had worked for or were still working for the company. The employees and their families were proud of the company, relied on it for their livelihoods and were themselves loyal customers of the company's products and shops.

The local radio station was sure their listeners would be interested in the prospects for future employment from a main board director.

In the course of the interview the HR director was asked if he shopped at the company's own retail outlets. His reply was broadcast for everyone to hear – *he didn't go into his own shops as he didn't want to rub shoulders with "the great unwashed".*

Both of these men were leaders. Both were being paid to foster the long-term interests of their company and its shareholders. And both did enormous harm to that company's morale – and its public profile with investors and consumers – with casual comments.

Both men were fortunate that their comments didn't attract widespread publicity or they could have created their own "Ratner effect". This is the description used for thoughtless, casual statements and their repercussions, first seen following a single speech made by Gerald Ratner. Within seconds, his attempt at humour set off a chain of events that would destroy his own company.

In 1991, Ratner was the CEO of a highly successful UK jewellers that he had built up over years. When invited to make his first speech to the Institute of Directors, he chose to describe his products as tacky and "total crap". The press and his customers were unforgiving. The company's share value dropped by £500m in a matter of days and Ratner lost his job within eighteen months. The brand no longer exists.

How can things go so wrong?

WHAT YOU SAY SHOWS HOW YOU THINK

In the great scheme of things, you may think the example about the HR director referring to "the great unwashed" is not so bad. You may wonder why I have chosen that story to emphasise. Nothing happened. The leader was crass but got away with it and there were no consequences like Ratner's. And you would be right. There are far larger scandals and examples of appalling leadership that have rightly been publicised. Even as I am writing this book, the founder of Papa Johns has had to resign from his own business after being accused of racism; and the head of people at Uber has resigned after failing to tackle racial discrimination, a year after Uber's founder left accused of gender discrimination and harassment. In fact even a cursory search shows widespread accusations of systemic bullying, harassment, discrimination, corporate self-interest etc. in organisations as diverse as universities, hospital trusts, sport governing bodies and charities as well as commercial businesses. Even the behaviour of Members of Parliament at the House of Commons is in the news at the moment!

All of these examples are appalling and rightly feeling the glare of publicity if true. These practices are never acceptable and the respective leadership should rightly be censured and taken to task if the accusations are proven.

But bad though these examples are, they usually impact a small number of people and get dealt with because of their shocking nature and the resultant uproar from publicity. Action gets taken.

There are far more problems that never get reported. There are less shocking but no less damaging leadership behaviours which never get reported and never have action taken to address them. Behaviours that are not necessarily illegal and not so grossly offensive that they attract publicity or consequences. But behaviours which are insidious and by their repetitive nature begin to severely impact on large numbers of employees, their welfare and their performance over time. And that is the subject of this book – not the scandals but the steady drip of poisonous attitudes and behaviours that company leadership teams inflict on their people.

Here are some real-life examples of what I mean:

o   Vernon, the group board director, who invented data to argue his business case for extra resources and berated a country director for a sales performance that was actually the reverse of what Vernon claimed.

o   Emily, the head of department, who thought it appropriate to give a senior manager's annual appraisal to him in front of his team and colleagues in an open-plan office.

o   Brian, the managing director, who took a week of sick leave every autumn half term for years as "I work so many antisocial hours I deserve more holiday".

o   Tony, the national sales director who encouraged his team of national account sales managers to treat the monthly promotion meetings as a sport to humiliate brand managers and ridicule their latest proposals.

o   Quentin, the category manager, who gave a graduate a poor review citing something that had happened ten months before but had never been mentioned at the time or any time since.

o   Nigel, the managing director, who regularly started meetings at 8.30am near his house when invitees had to travel over two hours to get to the venue.

o   Norman, the director, who started shouting and swearing at a senior manager because he did not agree with an action Norman demanded of him – in front of the manager's whole team in an open-plan office.

o   Edward, the purchasing director, who would regularly punish any of his senior managers if they disagreed with him by ignoring them and refusing to speak to them – for up to six months.

o Charlie, the senior manager, who only found out his job had been downgraded twelve months before when he tried to renew his company car and found he was no longer eligible.

o Steve, the managing director, who held a Christmas trading review until 7.30pm on a Friday night. He was thirty minutes away from home while some attendees had to travel up to four hours to their own homes.

o Clive, the senior manager with twenty years' impeccable service, who was forced into early retirement by his boss. He was made to work his full notice period for six months during which time his boss did not talk to him once.

o Brian, a rising star who turned down a prestigious position abroad as it would severely impact on his family. Brian was never considered for advancement again – hero to zero in the eyes of his bosses for turning down a promotion.

o Simon, the manager, who appointed a friend to a junior role in his team and promised a salary that he did not have the authority to give. When his friend found that his first pay cheque was short on what he expected, Simon assured him that it was a payroll error and faked e-mails from HR to back up his story.

o Julie, the store manager, whose best friend was always given preferential times for lunch breaks over all the other staff.

o Neville, the sales director, who falsely claimed authority from the CEO in demanding action from another department – unaware that the CEO had already made his actual decision clear to that department.

o The whole finance department of managers, who would agree to requests from other departments with no intention of carrying them out as they resented the extra workload.

o Simon, the CEO, on a conference call with senior managers, who described the managing director of a sister business unit as a "complete idiot".

- Carl, the marketing director of a team of twenty-four people, who left a business after four years and destroyed every file in his office so that the handover to his successor was just a stapler and some loose change left in the drawer.

- Chris, the supply chain director, who tried to play golf every time his CEO was out of the head office – and actively tried to encourage other directors to join him.

- Nick, the sales director, who regularly barged into other people's meetings without knocking or an apology. He would simply start a conversation with whoever he wanted information from at the time.

- Victor, the group board director, who routinely answered e-mails during the presentations of quarterly business reviews that had taken weeks to prepare at his request. He would then ask for parts of the presentation to be repeated as he had been too distracted to take notice first time.

- Lauren, the marketing manager, who gave suppliers falsified weekly sales and distribution reports, claiming returns on their promotion investment, for promotions that had never taken place. She was using their promotions budgets to simply inflate profits so she could gain her bonus.

- Eddie, the technical expert, who claimed he had ordered laboratory tests on a product and gave weekly updates on progress for months, including progress through customs, before finally admitting he had never commissioned the test in the first place.

- Liam, the sales director, who boasted to a new graduate how he falsified his sales figures routinely as a sales rep to get his bonuses.

- Natalie, the director, who refused to countersign payments as was required by the auditors of the whole operational board, a mind-numbing and time-consuming weekly task which made little commercial sense so she avoided doing it – meaning that all her fellow directors had to pick up her share as well.

- Pauline, the director, who would simply "forget" requests for information in case it was used to critique her own or her department's performance and decision-making processes.
- Simon, the board director, who booked out his diary "for interviews in London" when actually taking advantage of supplier hospitality at Wimbledon. A junior manager had booked holiday and paid to go to the tennis where he encountered the director. When challenged, the director justified himself saying, "You all do it".
- Lauren, the store manager, who dressed down her sales staff for not hitting targets but spent hours on Facebook and dating sites, in front of them, each working day.
- Dave, the pub manager, who held his forty staff to dress code standards but would be in the pub on his days off in a singlet and tracksuit bottoms drinking with regulars.
- Tim, the head of operations, who took the lead in the presentation of a new concept to board directors. He presented the work as if he had developed the thinking, despite only having a tangential role, to the frustration of the real project managers who were present in the meeting.
- Nial, the managing director, who asked questions in a concept review and repeatedly talked over the experts who tried to answer with their rationale, as it was at odds with his prejudices.
- Claire, the managing director, who disliked a business case as it didn't agree with what she wanted to do. Despite a thorough investigation of the facts and a detailed analysis being presented, she ended up saying, "The trouble with your research is you must be asking the wrong people the wrong questions." She insisted on the course of action she wanted despite no evidence to back it up.

And the list could go on and on. All of these examples are true. This list is by no means exhaustive and nor is it taken from one business alone. These issues are widespread and present in most businesses and every layer of management.

You may think some of these examples are literally incredible, that it is beyond believable that people behave in this way. I know they actually happened.

Or you may think also that some of these examples are petty and not even worth relaying. What's the big deal? Well let's examine that.

Every example impacts on a colleague or the reputation of the business. Every example breaks the most important thing you want to have with your leaders – trust. And the behaviours exposed show some of the least attractive and basest of human behaviours:

Lying; disrespect; humiliation; cowardice; fraud; unfairness; passive-aggression; childishness; hypocrisy; favouritism; laziness; deceit; game-playing; cheating; selfishness; bullying; skiving; emotional and psychological abuse.

This is the behaviour of the Casual Leaders and Casual Managers. Casual behaviours; casual mindsets. Casual abuse of their responsibility.

Casual Leaders do not take their role seriously and fail to reflect on their behaviours and impact on their colleagues. Casual Leaders fail to take personal responsibility for how they think, what they say and what they do. Casual Leaders damage the esteem of their position and their colleagues by unconcernedly promoting their selfish agendas. Casual Leaders damage the company by: setting the wrong example; preventing colleagues from advancing the business agenda; eroding colleagues' confidence and self-esteem; frustrating progress; choking ambition and initiative; silencing alternative opinions and strangling debate; forcing colleagues to protect themselves; destroying engagement.

And the worst thing about Casual Leadership? None of the behaviours above were censured. None of the behaviours led to consequences for that leader. Their behaviour was accepted by their line managers and by their peers and so they went on to routinely repeat those behaviours – again, and again, and again!

BEWARE THE CASUAL LEADERS
THEY LEAVE CASUALTIES WHEREVER THEY GO

In my view, most of these people were neither mad nor bad (and that may not always be true as we shall examine later in the book). Many of them were competent individuals but they still behaved poorly. They were Casual Leaders who did not take personal responsibility for their words or actions. And many of them would agree if forced to reflect on the legitimacy of their behaviours in an objective way. The things that unite them though are a poor level of self-awareness of their behaviour and its impact, poor emotional intelligence, and a lack of perspective.

WHAT CASUAL LEADERS LACK

WHAT YOU SAY SHOWS HOW YOU THINK

o   It is you alone who is responsible for what you say. Saying something good or bad is due to your cognitive processes. If you are only thinking of yourself, you are likely to say selfish things. If you think you are more gifted than others, you will risk coming across as patronising or arrogant.

WHAT YOU THINK DICTATES HOW YOU FEEL

o   No one can make you angry or frustrated or sad; those are decisions that you have made. It is the way you process what is going on around you and the inputs from others that determines how you decide to feel. Your feelings are a subconscious process showing how you think.

WHAT YOU THINK AND FEEL DICTATES HOW YOU ACT

o   "But I did it without thinking" is literally impossible. You may not be aware of thinking; it may have taken microseconds and appear instinctive; it may have been an unconscious process; but you cannot say or do anything without triggering a thought process. You may not have thought through how your actions appear to others or what the consequences might be but there is no action without thought.

YOUR ACTIONS DEMONSTRATE YOUR INNERMOST BELIEFS

- If you do not believe in honesty, you will have no problem lying. If you do not believe in equality, you will happily be a racist or a misogynist. If you do not believe in merit, you will see nothing wrong with patronage and favouritism. If you believe "the ends justify the means" you will happily play games, be manipulative and have a secret agenda.
- And if you have not thoroughly examined your innermost beliefs, if you behave on instinct alone and have not consciously decided who you want to be, you could be doing all of this subconsciously.
- The irony is that the Casual Leader is most probably a victim as well – a victim of themselves.

Casual Leaders not only lack this self-awareness. They lack perspective on society as a whole. I cannot believe that I have to write this section. But sometimes, if you think something does not need to be said, then you have to say it – or you are just working from an assumption. And clearly Casual Leaders are missing something or they would not behave as they do.

At the most basic, employees are just ordinary human beings like ourselves. Self-determining, independent, autonomous adults like you and me. With the same hopes and fears, needs and desires, anxieties, and capacity for love. And no matter how much we may think we are unique, or hope we may be a little bit special, we all know deep down inside that we are *no* more unique than anyone else. We have no greater right to feel safe, be respected, be free, be treated with fairness, have dignity, have choices, make mistakes, be irresponsible, be happy, be free to laugh, or to breathe in oxygen, than anyone else. In fact, this was the basis for the United Nations Universal Declaration of Human Rights when published in 1948. Everyone, everywhere, should have the same basic human rights – regardless of faith, nationality, race, gender, sexual orientation, status or age.

The Casual Leader seems to have lost this humility. So what grandiose sense of self-importance, what belief in their own superiority, what puffed-up ego, allows so many managers and directors in organisations to believe that they can treat others with disdain? Why is it that some leaders think they can disregard colleagues in their own organisation, such as the cleaners or porters or administrative clerks? Why is it that some leaders think they can patronise or belittle or intimidate colleagues just because their status is lower in the hierarchy of the organisation? What state of mind allows them to think they need not contribute to an efficient, supportive, harmonious culture in their own organisation?

How can Casual Leaders be so shameless when their actions are so shameful? Is it just lack of self-awareness? Lack of perspective? Or is there something more sinister going on?

THE SOCIAL CONTRACT

Towards the end of the twentieth century, the acclaimed sociologist Professor Morris Massey mapped out how each of us developed our own sense of the basic rules of how to live in reasonable harmony with other people. He called this process the development of values.

Not for the first time in researching this book, I was disappointed by the range of terms and definitions to pinpoint the precise meaning of words. And as we will see later, I think a number of commentators confuse meanings, especially of "values" and "integrity".

For some commentators, "value" is about monetary worth such as wealth or financial stability; for others it is about esteem and status. Others confuse values with morals or ethics. And for some values mean concepts such as motivational drivers, creativity, achievement, health, ambition, being the best, continuous learning, entrepreneurialism, family, initiative, job security, personal fulfilment, risk-taking etc. But these are not the values that I shall be talking about. For me, values are not things, states, ambitions, aspirations, motivations, skills, natural ability or mind sets that you may value or admire personally. The definition of values that I shall use throughout this book is the basic rules of how to live in reasonable harmony with other people. It's all about social beliefs that drive our behaviours and attitudes to build trust and encourage co-operation.

These rules, or values, are how independent, autonomous adults make sense of society and develop a sense of right and wrong, good and bad, in the way we treat and interact with other independent, autonomous adults. I like to think of this as our unspoken Social Contract between each and every one of us.

According to Massey, we each go through three distinct development phases to realise our values (or Social Contract):

o **Phase 1: The Imprint Period**
   Typically this is up to the age of seven years old, as we start life as essentially pre-moral. Our instincts are effectively Machiavellian and selfish; we do whatever we want to achieve our goals. However, as children, we are absorbing everything around us and accepting much of it as true, especially if it comes from our parents. And we start to develop an understanding of what is right and wrong.

NB It is in this period when an early formation of trauma can begin and it can lead to stunted emotional growth such as psychopathic tendencies.

o **Phase 2: The Modelling Period**
Between the ages of eight and thirteen years old we start to actively copy conventional values from parents and teachers, and even from religious leaders. No longer blindly accepting of right or wrong, we are exploring and experimenting with the concepts of good and bad.

o **Phase 3: The Socialisation Period**
This is the stage throughout our teenage years and into young adulthood at twenty-one years. We are increasingly influenced by our peers and outside influencers such as the media or role models, turning to and adopting their conventional values that seem most valid to us. It is by this time that we have established the basic rules for harmonious co-existence – or, as I call it, our Social Contract.

However, at this stage we will follow those rules only so long as we think we need to. We will still break these values occasionally, especially if we feel threatened or we think that no one will see us doing it.

According to Massey, only a few people will develop such a high regard for their values that it becomes an integral part of their being. When people are truly principled, they stick to their values come what may. They do not break these values even when no one is watching or even if it is not in their own self-interest. These are principled people whose values have become an absolute part of their identity. People such as Mahatma Gandhi, Martin Luther King or Nelson Mandela.

Why does this matter? The vast majority of employees are over twenty-one years old and will be already independent, self-determining, autonomous adults. By now, they have already developed a set of values that set out their belief in the right and wrong way to treat others or be treated themselves. They have already developed their own view of the Social Contract.

The Social Contract we develop is unique to ourselves and is unwritten. However, there must be elements that are universal, as they have to be reciprocated. Why else would we determine that these are the values or rules by which we should live to establish a reasonable harmony with other people?

These values go beyond just the letter of the law to the spirit of the law. They may pay homage to a country's traditions or religious teachings or tribal customs. And that is why there are variations and it is so difficult to pin down an accurate and universal list of what they might contain. What might be true of a First World technological country may not be true of a less-developed country. What might be true of one religious denomination may not be true of another. The concerns of one generation may not be reflected in another.

However, any universal list of values shared by everyone in their Social Contract is likely to include concepts of the following:

Honesty, respect, dignity, equality, the right to feel safe, fairness, privacy, civility, courtesy, compassion for the vulnerable, tolerance, consideration, self-control, commitment, humility, gratitude, responsibility, accountability, dependability.

These values are some of the rules (or beliefs, attitudes and behaviour) that most people would agree are the best way to live in reasonable harmony with other people in any society. They are the rules by which we live and which we hope are reciprocated by others. We live by them with our neighbours and within our neighbourhoods. We live by them when we travel: by car, by train, in airports. We live by them in every social setting:

at the cinema, in the theatre, in bars or restaurants. We live by them when we meet strangers or friends. We live by them when we interact with people in authority, such as the police or school teachers, but also when we are being served by people such as plumbers, cleaners, shop workers or waiting staff. And we teach them to our children as we know without these rules we would live in fear of each other or in anarchy.

NB Some commentators claim that these may be supplemented by other so-called personal values from the culture in which people have grown up. In the USA these might reflect the ideology of the American Dream (liberty, freedom of expression, work ethic, patriotism etc.) while in the UK they might reflect different cultural concerns (protecting the environment, civic responsibility, loyalty etc.). However, as I shall show later, I don't believe many of these are values. Instead, commentators are confusing these concepts with drivers or motivations behind our behaviours or competencies that we prize within the workplace.

In the next graphic, I will compare some of the expectations we have from our Social Contract with those behaviours we actually encounter at work from managers and colleagues. The values that we hold dear as a reasonable way to live in harmony with others are thrown into stark comparison with the reality that so many people experience. No wonder people get frustrated, disheartened and disengaged!

The Values of the Social Contract	Some of the Behaviours of the Casual Leader
Honesty	Lying, Deceit, Fabrication, Fake News
Respect	Disrespect
Dignity	Humiliation
Equality	Favouritism
The Right to Feel Safe; Compassion for the Vulnerable	Bullying, Intimidation, Emotional Blackmail
Fairness	Taking Credit due to Others, Blame
Privacy	Ignoring Boundaries
Civility, Courtesy	Rudeness, Ignorance
Tolerance	Judgement, Criticism
Self-Control	Anger, Shouting, Volatility
Consideration	Entitlement, Disregard
Humility	Boasting, Arrogance, Patronisation
Gratitude	Lack of Recognition
Commitment	Shirking, Vagueness, Cheating
Dependability	Unreliability, Flightiness, Capriciousness

THE WORK CONTRACT

The days of serfdom, homage to the lord of the manor and slave-trading have long gone. Employees choose to work for an employer and it is a bartering system. Effectively they are saying that, for their livelihood, they are prepared to barter their expertise and their skill for a number of hours a week in exchange for the employer's cash. And the vast majority will end up signing a Work Contract making the arrangement legally binding on both parties.

Typically, in the UK the contract looks something like this:

o   37.5 hours a week
o   Normally between 9am–5pm, Monday to Friday
o   At a specified location
o   In exchange for £x per annum

And, there are usually all sorts of sinecures which allow management discretion: working outside those hours sometimes; or at a different location occasionally; or overtime or antisocial hours arrangements; or an incentive structure over and above the agreed salary related to performance.

It is legally binding but it is also a choice and it is voluntary on both parties. Implicitly when an employee and employer sign this contract they are saying that this is a fair exchange at that point in time. Both parties have a stake in the arrangement and both parties are fully engaged.

So far so good. And the implications are clear. The employee cannot say, "I only want to work half those hours and still be paid the same." Nor can the employer say, "I want you to work twice as many hours for the same amount of money," or "You have worked your hours but I am only going to pay you half of what has been agreed."

And they all lived happily ever after? Of course not!

In my experience, most employees start employment highly engaged. From day one, they are on the ball. They are eager to make the right impression, they are keen to do a good job, they want to be accepted by colleagues and respected by their line manager for the quality of their output. In fact, I believe most people want to finish the week knowing they have worked hard, it has been appreciated and that they deserve the money they have earned as they are contributing to the success of the company.

So how do we explain why so many people become disengaged? How do these eager beavers turn into jobsworths, or sluggish workers just going through the routine with no pace or enthusiasm? Why do they no longer bring the best version of themselves to work but instead a pale imitation just serving out the working week?

I have seen many managers who have blamed the workers but have never looked in the mirror and examined themselves. And the truth is that these eager beavers change because of the way they have been led by the Casual Leaders.

At the heart of the problem is the lack of social perception by the Casual Leader. What they fail to understand is that this is a voluntary agreement that has been entered into.

At no stage did the employees sign a Work Contract saying that it trumped or superseded their expectation of the Social Contract.

No employee has ever signed a contract stating that, "I will give you Y hours for X money AND you can disrespect me. Or humiliate me. Or lie to me. Or treat me unfairly. Or discriminate against me. Or shout at me. Or intimidate me. Or harass me. Or invade my privacy. Or be rude to me." No one has ever volunteered for that and no one has ever signed a legally binding document agreeing to that. So why does the Casual Leader think this is ever going to be acceptable? (More on that later in the book.)

The expectations of the Social Contract exist no matter what type of Work Contract is in place. It does not matter if the employee is contracted out to another supplier. It does not matter if the employee is on a zero-hours contract. It does not matter if the worker is on a short-term project or employed on a consultancy basis. All these people are employees in some form and should have their Social Contract and Work Contract recognised and be managed accordingly by the leaders.

And, there are other poor behaviours from the Casual Leader which are less obvious.

For example, it is well documented that employees require a clear declaration of their role and its responsibilities to understand their remit and know what a good job looks like. And that they require continual feedback so that they can understand how they are performing to expectations. So most reputable human resources departments have put in formal processes and documentation to achieve these aims. These take the shape of: job descriptions, hierarchy charts, frequent one-to-one meetings with line managers, structured appraisals, formal objective-setting, etc. In my experience, these processes are time-consuming but thoroughly worthwhile. However, they are rarely policed and tracked. And so, the Casual Managers take a sloppy approach, doing the minimum they can get away with. It is not unusual to find job descriptions and hierarchy charts are out of date and inaccurate; that one-to-one feedback sessions are not taking place, negating any timeliness in structured critique of performance; that appraisals do not happen, or are rushed and lack substance; and that objectives are late and vague.

Further, many employees are happy to work extra hours over and above their contract, particularly those that have overtime or incentive benefits. They have pride in their work, want to do a good job and can see the organisation's needs. Even if they don't get directly compensated, many are keen to see through a job well done and will occasionally work extra time to ensure this happens. But it is entirely voluntary and I have often seen the Casual Leader abuse this goodwill, demanding this extra work and depriving employees of family or leisure time. It has happened to me and my colleagues. Often we have been expected to get up at 3am to fly to a meeting in Europe, or expected to work late into the early hours without warning, or had a work meeting booked in over an entire weekend with no consultation, or been expected to attend a conference and be away from home all week. Once, it was suggested to me that I should abandon my young family in the middle of our annual two-week holiday and fly back to brief analysts in Birmingham for just four hours!

The Good Leader knows that he needs his employees to be fresh and rested. After all, he is relying on the quality of their thinking or manual input. It is common sense that, if people are exhausted mentally or physically, they will not perform to the highest standards they are capable of; mistakes and inefficiencies will happen, opportunities and momentum will be lost. The Good Leader ensures quality not quantity and takes responsibility for their people's well-being by ensuring that work-streams are manageable and that the environment is safe, healthy and comfortable. So why do so many leaders fail to take responsibility for their people's well-being? Why do they make such demands that it leads to unhealthy lifestyles such as missing meals or excessive hours? Why do they think it acceptable to expect replies to e-mails or texts over the weekend or when employees are on holiday? Why do they insist on restricting the expenses budget, compromising on travel and accommodation, rather than ensuring employees are rested and relaxed in comfort? It is the frequency of these expectations that causes dissent, particularly if the experience is not engaging and essential, or when the time is not used efficiently and is wasted. All of these threaten the work–life balance of most people. MOST PEOPLE WORK TO LIVE; THEY DON'T LIVE TO WORK – which the Casual Leader frequently forgets.

The moment Casual Leaders presume they can demand commitment outside of the Work Contract is the moment they overstep their authority. This is called "entitlement" – the unreasonable belief that they have the inherent right to something.

What was agreed initially by both parties as a fair exchange of time and skills for cash suddenly shifts into an unbalanced arrangement. Inevitably the employee becomes disaffected and resentful OR decides this voluntary arrangement is no longer satisfactory and leaves the company. And when Casual Leaders disregard the Social Contract, as well as the Work Contract, it is a recipe for disaster. They retain the least confident and disaffected employees, while losing the most capable and those with the most self-esteem.

And the irony is that most leaders are actually employees too. The sole exception to this rule is the owner-entrepreneur.

So, if there are any shareholders, every layer of an organisation consists of employees. From the chairman and CEO, through the directors and management levels, down to the clerical and manual roles. All are employees – and all have expectations of the Social and Work Contracts. What is it about the Casual Leaders that allows them to forget this?

And why is anyone employed at all? The truth is that the employee must serve an indispensable and vital function for the organisation. There is no other explanation after a generation of downsizing, redundancies, layoffs, outsourcing etc. If the employee did not serve a vital function then they would no longer be employed in the first place.

The inference from this is that an employee either already has the skills or has the potential to develop the skills to serve a vital function. With experience they should only execute that function ever faster and more effectively. So they are vital to both the current and also the future performance of the organisation. That makes them valuable and worthy of attention. So why do so many Casual Leaders miss the obvious even when they desire it for themselves? Why do they dismiss people as replaceable and not see the opportunity costs of letting someone go – the cost of new recruitment, the loss of time and management focus devoted to that process, the lower levels of productivity until someone has been familiarised and got into an effective pattern of work?

WHAT MAKES A LEADER AND WHO DO YOU NEED TO BE?

There are some fairly irreverent theories on what is a Leader! And they show a sceptical attitude to leadership quality that has been voiced for decades.

In 1969, Laurence J. Peter and Raymond Hull published *The Peter Principle*. This principle asserts that a person can be so competent at their job that they will be successively promoted until they reach a level of incompetence. And then they remain stuck at that level for the rest of their career – perennially incompetent in leading parts of the organisation.

In 1995, Scott Adams promoted the idea of "The Dilbert Principle". Author of the wonderfully cynical take on corporate life though the Dilbert cartoons, Adams had his hero Dogbert state "leadership is nature's way of removing morons from the productive flow". Adams explains his principle as stating that companies tend to systematically promote their least competent employees to management to limit the amount of damage they are capable of doing. "In many cases the least competent, least smart people are promoted, simply because they're the ones you don't want doing actual work. You want them ordering the doughnuts and yelling at people for not doing their assignments—you know, the easy work."

Both works were intended to be satirical but I am sure bring a smile to your face. For me, Scott Adam's thesis does not resonate with my experience in my career. It is too cynical and, paradoxically, anarchical. However, I do believe that I have seen evidence of the Peter Principle at work and that it is a real phenomenon. Sometimes an organisation has grown quickly from acquisition, or technology has been embraced, or the market has developed into different channels of distribution, creating demands of the leadership team which outstripped their previous competency. One company I know lacked the courage to tackle the problem of leaders exposed like this and instead of demoting them or firing them would move them into "special projects" or even promote them into side-line businesses where they could not harm the core activities of the central business!

Central to both principles are some core assumptions about leadership and what a leader is. They both assume that a leader is within a hierarchy of management and therefore has some responsibility for people reporting into them. They both confine themselves just to the competency of doing a job. Neither expand on *who a leader is*.

There is certainly no shortage in commentary trying to answer *what is a leader?* And we will all have our favourite.

o "Leadership is a development of a clear and complete system of expectations in order to identify, evoke and use the strengths of all resources in the organization the most important of which is people." – J.D. Batten, *Tough-Minded Leadership*

o "Leadership is a function of knowing yourself, having a vision that is well communicated, building trust among colleagues, and taking effective action to realize your own leadership potential." – Warren Bennis

o   "People ask the difference between a leader and a boss...
    The leader works in the open, and the boss in covert. The
    leader leads, and the boss drives." – Theodore Roosevelt
o   "Leadership is defined as the process of influencing the
    activities of an organized group toward goal achievement."
    – Rauch & Behling
o   "Leadership is the art of influencing others to their maximum
    performance to accomplish any task, objective or project." –
    W.A. Cohen, *The Art of a Leader*
o   "The function of leadership is to produce more leaders, not
    more followers." – Ralph Nadar

The mechanics of leadership are well articulated by many
commentators. And there are consistent themes from many of
them:

o   A leader has a vision of what needs to be done and can
    align their own and their team's objectives with that of the
    strategy.
o   They have an energy which they can generate amongst
    other people.
o   They are constantly learning to improve their own
    knowledge and skills.
o   They go beyond communicating and engage colleagues.
o   They stretch themselves and others with realistic targets
    that are a challenge.
o   They support colleagues through coaching, mentoring and
    monitoring the demands of work-streams against the time
    available.
o   They encourage teamwork through communication and
    collaborative information-sharing – both as a team leader
    and as a team player.
o   They give recognition to other people's contributions.
o   They listen first, examine alternative views, and talk last.

o   They praise achievements by others.
o   They deliver results by delegating authority and encourage ownership by allowing people to use their own judgement.
o   They deliver efficiency through an ability to prioritise work and by streamlining processes, never wasting time for anyone.
o   And they go on to measure progress by tracking goals being delivered.
o   They are completer–finishers of the tasks tackled.

More recent commentators have expanded on these mechanics. In his excellent book *Leadership Plain and Simple*, Steve Radcliffe advocates that anyone at any level of an organisation can be a leader – both at work and in their domestic lives. For him, leaders see the widest context rather than just their part. He encourages developing self-awareness via a support network to provide feedback on "impact felt" rather than "impact intended". He argues that it is a set of skills to be learned through conscious practice.

Other commentators take this broader and more holistic view. They see a societal impact and are more humanist in their approach. Ken Blanchard, in *Gung Ho! – How to Motivate the People in Any Organisation*, introduces the concept of "worthwhile work" and understanding how your job benefits society as a whole. He sees that people who feel respected, listened to and valued will respond to the challenge of delivering the goal and become leaders in their own right, going on to encourage the achievement of others. Simon Sinek builds on these themes with his brilliant book *Leaders Eat Last*. He believes that anyone can be a leader at any level of an organisation. He advocates building a sense of safety through a "circle of trust" to protect the well-being of your colleagues and believes that this comes through empathy. While he supports the mechanics of leadership, Sinek is clear that it is all about people: taking responsibility for their well-being and giving commitment to fellow human beings.

When I first read Simon Sinek's book I found myself smiling, clapping and cheering out loud! If you have not read it, do so. It should be compulsory reading for any adult and adopted into the reading syllabus for schools! At last, I thought, someone who is actually talking about what I think are the most important things that make up a leader. But even Sinek does not go far enough and talk about *who a leader is* – who you are and what you have to be. In fact, there are some observations by Sinek that I go onto disagree with later in the book. More on that later.

So there are an enormous number of commentators and some universal themes on the mechanics of leadership. At least a few argue that it is not confined to a business or artificial organisational hierarchy. And there is some consensus that anyone can be a leader but that leadership has to be learned. Whereas we established in the last chapter that everyone is an employee at work, we can now see that everyone can be a leader whether at work or not. But no one as yet as talked about who a leader is.

We have already touched on a number of themes on what creates a leader: competency, vision, energy, empathy, a communicator.

BUT TO BE LEADER, WHO DO YOU NEED TO BE?

The Attributes of a Good Leader	The Attributes of a Casual Leader
Has vision into society and all the parts of the organisational strategy	Vision is limited to their task
Personal energy	Lacklustre
Personal competency and a commitment to continuous learning	Complacency
Engages through compelling communication	Tells and orders people what to do
Challenges themselves and others	Criticises others; defends themselves
Supports others	Sets unrealistic demands and ignores development needs
Facilitates teamwork	Works for themselves
Gives recognition	Takes credit
Listens to and examines alternative views	Talks over the top of others and crushes dissent
Praises others	Takes others for granted
Delegates authority and encourage ownership	Takes every decision and thinks they know best
Prioritises	Treats everything with the same importance; nothing is sequential
Measures progress	Decides what success looks like after the event
Completer–finisher	Creator of chaos, dysfunction and frustration

So who is a leader? I am an enormous fan of Peter Drucker, whom I would contend is the most eminent commentator on business management theory and practice. And it is he whom I would first look to for inspiration on this subject. However, Drucker was notoriously sceptical about leadership and for years distrusted the concept, preferring to talk about managers. This is in part due to his dislike of the admiration of charisma as a leadership quality. "The three most charismatic leaders in this century inflicted more suffering on the human race than almost any trio in history: Hitler, Stalin, and Mao," he said.

In later years, Drucker relented his previous views and gave us these two famous quotes:

> "THE ONLY DEFINITION OF A LEADER IS
> SOMEONE WHO HAS FOLLOWERS"

> "MANAGEMENT IS DOING THINGS RIGHT;
> LEADERSHIP IS DOING THE RIGHT THINGS"

At first glance, I was underwhelmed by these thoughts and took them as literal statements on people, responsibility and selecting the right business vision or strategy. But the more I understood Drucker, the more insightful I have found these quotes. For Drucker was not just an advocate of efficient working practices but a deeply principled man who believed in values and developing the potential of individuals who are your responsibility. And so I believe that at least part of what Drucker was advocating was leaders do the right things *by people* and that is why they have followers.

WHO IS A LEADER? A LEADER IS
A POSITIVE ROLE MODEL

A leader is someone whom we can look to and think they are an example worth imitating. They embody all the things that we value and respect. They are visible and they live their life by the values we expect of the Social Contract. They are competent and have all the skills and knowledge that we believe they need to execute their Work Contract. They literally lead by example. They do not *demand* respect because of their title or a place in an artificial hierarchy created for a work setting. They *command* respect because of who they are, their behaviours towards us and others, as well as their competency in their role.

None of these things come by accident. You cannot be a positive role model without a deep level of self-awareness and a strong conviction to values as being the right rules of behaviour to live in reasonable harmony with others. It is hard work to become and stay a decent human being; it requires a brutal honesty with yourself, a lot of soul-searching and an empathy for others. And it's even harder work when you are placed in a position of visibility such as the work environment, where everyone is aware of how you conduct yourself and how you behave towards others.

You do not become a positive role model by accident. It is a conscious process to develop that model of behaviour and you have to retain a constant awareness of situations to maintain it. If you have really examined your conscience and have developed deep convictions on values, you are halfway there, at least on the Social Contract. However, as Massey asserted, the majority of us will follow those rules only so long as we think we need to. We will still break these values occasionally, especially if we feel threatened or we think that no one will see us doing it. And at work there is little chance that no one will see us breaking values!

Developing values is little different from developing the other skills that we require to be considered competent at work. Martin Broadwell first articulated the "Four Stages of Learning" in 1969. He saw four stages which are often expressed as a pyramidal hierarchy:

1   **Unconscious Incompetence**
    You don't understand or know how to do something. You don't even have the knowledge of what you don't know; e.g. before you learn to drive, you do not know how to change gears or when to signal a change of direction. You have no understanding of the things you need to learn to be a safe driver.

2   **Conscious Incompetence**
    You lack knowledge but recognise the defect and learn from your mistakes; e.g. you take driving lessons from a qualified instructor. However, you keep clashing the car's gears or stalling the engine; or you find yourself approaching junctions at too high a speed.

3   **Conscious Competence**
    You have learned how to do something but you need to concentrate to do it well; e.g. you painstakingly look in the mirror before signalling and then changing direction.

4   **Unconscious Competence**
    You have developed so much skill from practice that it becomes second nature, and you instinctively do the right things in the right order. e.g. you drive automatically to your destination and cannot remember the journey afterwards but your passengers feel safe at all times.

As Massey argued that only a very few of us are truly principled, with values that are indelibly part of our character, then I contend that the four stages of learning to be a role model are actually of a circular nature and not a seamless one-way progression to Unconscious Competence. The fourth stage cannot be maintained without us lapsing back into the Unconscious Incompetence stage again. Keeping with the driving analogy, we become so blasé and complacent, our driving standards eventually slip, we drive with one hand on the steering wheel, don't look before we manoeuvre and go too fast in poor weather conditions!

THE CIRCLE OF COMPETENCY

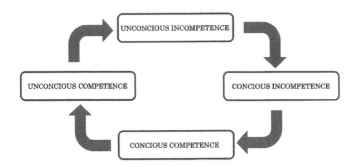

We are all required to stay supremely conscious of our values and of our behaviours at all times and reflect back on what we have done – preferably remedying mistakes – if we are to become positive role models.

So how do we explain the Casual Leaders? Clearly Casual Leaders are not positive role models. In fact they are the reverse – negative role models. Measured against this model they are in the Unconscious Incompetence phase and it is doubtful if they have ever progressed through the phases of learning, for their behaviour to be so ingrained and systemic. But how can we explain why they have allowed themselves to become like that?

On the surface, there are only three obvious explanations:

1   They have no understanding of the unacceptability of their behaviour – a lack of self-awareness.

2   They have no understanding of their impact on others –
a lack of empathy and emotional intelligence as they lack
perspective.
3   They believe their behaviour is acceptable as it emulates
their own role models, either consciously or unconsciously.

NB There is a fourth explanation, which we will explore in the
next section.

In my experience, it is a mixture of all three explanations.
Casual Leaders are the first to rail against the callous behaviours
of others towards them but fail to see that they behave in the
same way to others. They have no greater liking of being treated
with disrespect or of being disregarded than any of the rest of
us but they fail to reflect or be honest with themselves, let alone
own up to, apologise or correct their own behaviour. And the
main reason for this is that they are either consciously, or, more
likely, unconsciously copying patterns of behaviour learned
from their own role models.

ARE CASUAL LEADERS IN ADULT MODE?

In the 1950s, the psychiatrist Eric Berne developed his theory of transactional analysis, which still remains one of the staple influences on modern psychotherapy today. He wrote a number of articles and popular books presenting his theories, including *The Games People Play,* and was a prime influence on Thomas Harris, who wrote the best-known book on transactional analysis, *I'm OK, You're OK.*

Berne's theories were based on the ideas of Freud but, instead of focussing on personality, he felt that insight could be best gained from the way people interact socially. He called these interactions "transactions" and mapped the three ego-states that are the source of people's behaviour: parent, adult *and* child. He argued that, at any given time, a person experiences and then manifests his thoughts, feelings and behaviours through these three learned ego-states. And these are the role models of behaviour that govern our interactions with others.

Typically the theory of transactional analysis and the three ego-states are explained as follows:

o   Our adult patterns of life were determined through childhood experiences.

o   Without self-awareness, we will copy the patterns we learnt from role models such as parents or repeat the behaviour strategies that worked for us as a child.

o   We have to be aware of, and consciously construct, an intelligent thought-processing system in order for us to achieve an *adult ego-state*. This is the only state that can make predictions about emotional reactions and control them. And it is the only state in which one can achieve an objective appraisal of reality and of our reaction to others. This is the state from which we can base reasonable behaviour and conversations – because they are literally based on reason!

o   If we do not, we might unconsciously mimic the behaviours of our *parent ego-state* (our own parents or other parental figures). For example, shouting out of frustration, as that is what we learnt was an acceptable way to behave when we were children. There are sub-structures of this ego-state. So there are *nurturing parent* states that give permission or security; and there are *critical parent* states that are negative and undermining.

o   Or we might continue to repeat the thought patterns and behaviours learnt from our childhood – our *child ego-state*. For example, reacting to a bad evaluation at work by sulking or pouting. Again, there are sub-structures of this ego-state; the *free child* may have natural and uninhibited behaviours, or the *adapted child* might be a people-pleaser in an effort to get approval or recognition.

The theory explains that we will each approach a social interaction from one of these three ego-*states and* we will instinctively react to whichever ego-state we detect is being used by the person we are interacting with. So if we think we are being talked down to by a parent our first reaction will be to adopt a successful child strategy learned from our past. Similarly, we might be overwhelmed by a decision and adopt a childlike ego to solicit a parental response from the other. And in the course of any interaction we might flow from one ego-state to another as we converse.

AN ILLUSTRATION OF TRANSACTIONAL ANALYSIS

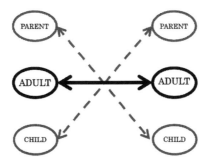

The challenge for each of us is to develop our adult ego-state, particularly at work. And then to maintain that no matter what ego-state is being presented back to us. Our job is to try and encourage our colleague to join us in their own adult ego-state. And that is how the interaction can remain reasonable and objective.

How many times have you left a meeting and described someone as having "lost it", "thrown his dummy out of the pram" or "thrown his toys out the window"?

In my opinion, transactional analysis (TA) gives us the key to understand what we have seen and just joked about. TA shows that, in those circumstances, that person was not in adult mode at the time. You could have been dealing with someone who was showing their child ego-state or their parent ego-state. It may be hard to believe that a fifty-year-old, ex-rugby-playing family man was literally behaving like a child at the time, but that is what was going on!

The power of role models is often talked about in the media, usually with commentary about sports idols or pop stars. And of course we can all have heroes that we look up to and perceive as a positive role model to follow and copy. However, the power that role models exert over us can be subtle and we may not recognise or acknowledge it. We do not always make a conscious choice to follow models of behaviour; we may be slavishly yet subconsciously following poor or inappropriate models.

Our formative years, as children, are a period when we are particularly powerless and vulnerable, and yet we soak up knowledge and influences like a sponge, trying to make sense of what is going on about us. When we grow up to be powerful adults, we may still be adopting strategies that were successful for us as powerless children or we may be subconsciously copying the poor behaviours and actions of authority figures like our parents. And that is cyclical through the generations, for your parents may well have done the same.

In his book *Leaders Eat Last*, Simon Sinek quotes my favourite poem.

> **"This Be the Verse" by Philip Larkin.**
> *They fuck you up, your mum and dad.*
> *They may not mean to, but they do.*
> *They fill you with the faults they had*
> *And add some extra, just for you.*
>
> *But they were fucked up in their turn*
> *By fools in old-style hats and coats,*
> *Who half the time were soppy-stern*
> *And half at one another's throats.*

I read this when I was still a teenager and I have always believed this poem shows an incredible insight into the human condition. It allowed me to understand and have compassion towards many of the formative figures of my childhood. It is also one of the reasons that I admire Simon Sinek himself; who could not like someone who quotes your favourite poem? However I do depart from one of Simon's arguments, which is that leaders should behave as parents to their employees. I understand the sentiment and that Simon was arguing for a duty of care towards employees as from a nurturing parent. And there are times, of course, when this is particularly appropriate. But, as TA shows, not everyone had such parental figures. Some had absent parents, others had ambivalent parents or even indulgent parents; and most frequently children grew up with critical parents instead.

Overall, I contend that while the nurturing parent can be appropriate, the most effective ego-state is that of adult, and Good Leaders treat their employees as adults too.

To illustrate my theory I shall return to a widely accepted set of criteria for Good Leaders: they *support* and they *challenge*.

The psychologist and educationalist Professor Nevitt Sanford is widely credited for first proposing the Support–Challenge Model in the 1950s and '60s. It was originally proposed to be a concept for developing student learning and is often expressed as a graph.

SANFORD'S SUPPORT CHALLENGE DYNAMIC

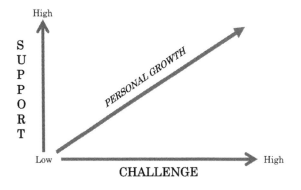

The central theory is that to optimise learning the environment requires variety, complexity and be impelling enough to force students to make decisions, whilst still being safe and protective enough to prevent too much anxiety. It is recognised that a delicate balance is required to avoid students from retreating from too much challenge or alternatively failing to develop due to receiving too much support, and is still used by many educational authorities today.

The model has been widely adopted by organisations to illustrate the building of capability for their employees. The thesis is that employees require both leadership support (e.g. training, coaching, mentoring) as well as the challenge of goal achievement and productivity to become high performers. One such illustration is below.

When the challenge is high but not balanced by sufficient support, the employees underperform as they feel so much anxiety that they feel stressed. Typically they are full of apprehension, concerned about protecting themselves in a hostile environment and prone to panic. Time is frittered away as they fear fierce criticism, or worse, so they are constantly watching their backs and covering their arses. This is a position of low trust!

BUSINESS SUPPORT CHALLENGE MATRIX

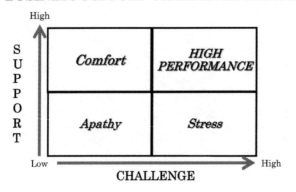

Conversely, if there is low challenge but lots of support, they underperform because they do not feel stretched, there are no deadlines and they have no stress at all. Time is frittered away at work as it is an environment which is full of ease and people stagnate. They may get lots of compassion and attention but there is no sense of achievement or accomplishment. They may feel engaged on a personal level but not with the organisation's needs and objectives. There is no progress towards a common goal.

The worst position is that of apathy: low challenge and low support. This is completely unproductive as no one cares about performance. This is an environment typified as full of inertia and boredom, low in optimism and drive, low in determination and progress, and low in engagement by leaders and employees.

The optimal position for high performance is an environment that sets challenging but realistic goals and objectives balanced by the right level of support. This support might come from coaching or mentoring; it might come from training or equipment; but it is most likely to come through close teamwork, high levels of information-sharing and co-operation, and a high degree of mutual respect. Opinions are aligned; the goal is clear; interdependencies are understood; everyone is committed to a common cause and feels valued; and everyone knows what success looks like. The work demands the best from each individual and they can feel accomplished as they make progress towards the goal. This position allows continuous learning, encourages innovation and appropriate risk-taking; it allows personal development and business or process renewal. This is an environment of high trust.

If we transpose transactional analysis onto the matrix we can see the impact of the leader on the employee. Each ego-state taken by the leader sets up and solicits a different response from the employee.

TRANSACTIONAL ANALYSIS IN THE MATRIX

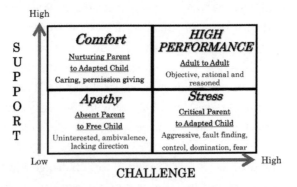

I have always found that, if as a leader you treat your colleagues and direct reports as adults, they will respond as adults! Of course this is not surprising. After all they function as independent, autonomous adults in their everyday lives outside of work. Why would they not behave like that inside work if allowed to do so?

But this is the trap so many organisations and Casual Leaders fall into. They continually take the position of a parent and frustrate the initiative and ability of their employees. Subconsciously or consciously, they assume a superiority rather than an authority as entitled from their rank or status and decide to patronise and belittle their colleagues.

The simplicity of this model is highly appealing to me and I have used it for years. I find you can easily map yourselves, colleagues, teams, whole departments or the complete organisation. So the next time you feel something does not add up in your workplace and you are dissatisfied with the boss, try mapping the organisation and ask yourself: are the leaders in adult mode?

NEITHER MAD NOR BAD

Earlier in the book, I made this assertion. But all may not be as it seems.

So far I have argued that the Casual Leader can be competent but may lack a sense of their position in society and the perspective which that brings. I have argued also that they may have a chronic lack of self-awareness and may not be in control of their inner dialogue, being slaves to their subconscious role models. But there is clearly a large problem of poor leadership out there, which is having a big impact on morale and therefore engagement and productivity.

A simple Google search for related topics in August 2018 yielded the following results on search terms:

1   Difficult people at work = 609 million results
2   Abuse at work = 573 million results
3   Good Leaders = 484 million results
4   Poor Leaders = 185 million results
5   Hate my boss = 173 million

Of course I don't pretend this is a serious piece of research but I do think that the scale of the issues is indicative of people's concerns. Could there be more than lack of perspective and low self-awareness going on?

It is well documented that one in four of us will suffer some sort of mental health issue in the course of our lives. These may take the form of depression, anxiety or phobias and, despite being common, have long been a taboo topic of discussion, even at home let alone in the workplace. With the support of the Royal Family, this issue is at last being publicised in the UK and the stigma surrounding mental health is being eroded.

However, what is less publicised are underlying personality disorders. These are recognised worldwide by psychiatrists and are far more common than most people would believe.

Before you start rolling your eyes, or letting your imagination run riot with images of Hannibal Lecter and straightjackets or other popular Hollywood images, you need to consider the nature of personality disorders. While at the extreme you do have highly exaggerated and antisocial behaviours, for the most part the behaviours are on a spectrum. For whatever reason, some people develop parts of their personality which make it difficult for them to live either with themselves or with other people. They seem unable to learn or cope with events that happen to them or cannot change their behaviours and reactions that cause the original problem. These are deeply ingrained ways of thinking and behaving that are inflexible and generally lead to impaired relationships with other people.

Psychiatrists have identified three broad clusters of personality disorder:

1 **Cluster A – Odd or Eccentric**
   This cluster includes three separate types: paranoid, schizoid and schizotypal personality disorders. They can dislike or be suspicious of contact with other people. Some can feel easily rejected while others are emotionally cold, have odd ideas and eccentric behaviours.

2   **Cluster B – Dramatic, Emotional or Erratic**
This is probably the largest cluster. Personality disorder types included in this cluster are: antisocial, borderline (or emotionally unstable), histrionic, and narcissistic. Many are self-centred and don't care about the feelings of others. They can have low feelings of guilt, difficulty in creating deep and meaningful relations, and be manipulative or exploitative of others.

I believe this cluster is the most likely to be encountered at work as behaviours can be less demonstrable and quite subtle across the spectrum and therefore people appear to be fully functioning in a social context.

3   **Cluster C – Anxious and Fearful**
This cluster includes personality disorders such as obsessive–compulsive, avoidant or dependent. Most behaviours tend to be passive and inward-looking. Sufferers tend to worry a lot, be sensitive to criticism, and be cautious and tentative with decision-making.

Estimates of personality disorder incidence in the general population vary widely but are still much higher than many may assume:

o   The Royal College of Psychiatrists quote that one in twenty (5%) of the general population may suffer from a personality disorder. In their education leaflet to the general public, they recognise that previous research studies had suggested it could be even higher at one in five (20%).
o   The British Journal of Psychiatry quotes a study of adults in Britain to show the prevalence of personality disorders at 4.4% of the population.
o   The US National Institutes of Health have quoted that 7.9% of Americans suffer from obsessive compulsive disorder,

6.2% from narcissistic personality disorder and 5.9% can suffer from borderline personality disorder. As some of these overlap, the journal *Innovations in Clinical Neuroscience* estimates that the general incidence of personality disorders in the US population is 9.7%, taken from a review of five separate clinical studies.

o The UK charity Mind says that recent NHS research in 2014 shows up to 3.3% of the general population may suffer from antisocial personality disorder and 2.4% from borderline personality disorder.

The sheer range of statistics shows how hard it is to detect and diagnose personality disorders accurately. Many of the symptoms exist in all of us. I recognise some of the characteristics in my own behaviours. I can be sensitive to criticism or get frustrated. I like detail and routines and can be selfish. I can get anxious or be preoccupied with detail. We all exhibit some of these thoughts and behaviours along a spectrum. And all of these are fine if they do not become extreme, entrenched or excessive in their influence on our behaviours to others. It is all about moderation and perspective. But most psychiatrists agree that personality disorders are a real phenomenon in everyday society and have a far higher prevalence than most of the general public would suppose.

So, before you scoff and dismiss the idea that you are sharing the workplace with people that could be diagnosed with a personality disorder, let's look at those statistics.

Even if we took the lowest estimate of 5%, it means in a small office of 400 people there could be up to twenty colleagues that are high up on the spectrum of a personality disorder. That's right – twenty! Even if we were to halve that number because we have blind faith in our recruitment policies and the excellence of our training. Even if were to halve it again in the belief we would have recognised someone as behaving with a personality disorder and exited them from the business. Even with those spurious assumptions in our own competence, in an office of 400 we would find five colleagues who had personality impairments bordering on a clinical diagnosis for a personality disorder. It does not seem so far-fetched now!

There have been many books and articles written on this very problem within the workplace over the years. For example in the *Harvard Business Review*: Michael Maccoby, "Narcissistic Leaders: The Incredible Pros, the Inevitable Cons" (Jan 2004) or Gardiner Morse, "Executive Psychopaths" (Oct 2004). In *Forbes*: Victor Lipman, "The Disturbing Link between Psychopathy and Leadership" (Apr 2013). There are also books such as Dr Martha Stout's *The Sociopath Next Door* or Paul Babiak & Robert Hare's *Snakes in Suits* or Dr George Simon's *In Sheep's Clothing: Understanding and Dealing with Manipulative People*.

So perhaps those difficult people at work are unreasonable because they cannot be reasoned with! Perhaps they are pathologically inclined to behave in ways that you find difficult or antisocial. Perhaps they are difficult to manage because they cannot manage themselves. And perhaps they achieve status within organisational hierarchies only to become Casual Leaders.

So let's explore the dynamics of just two personality disorders and see if you recognise these traits amongst your colleagues.

The narcissistic personality disorder at its extreme shows itself as a grandiose sense of self-importance, preoccupation with unlimited success and a belief that one is special and unique. There are other traits which may be more subtle:

o An overwhelming need for admiration.
o A lack of empathy for others and uncomfortable with people expressing their emotions.
o Independent, constantly looking out for enemies and sometimes paranoid under stress.

○ Selfish and aggressive pursuit of own goals.

○ Snobbish, disdainful or patronising attitudes.

○ A strong sense of entitlement.

○ Often envious of others and not easily impressed.

○ Sensitive to criticism and intolerant of dissent.

○ Highly manipulative or exploitative and can be charming to get their own way.

○ Highly distrustful and poor team workers.

○ Find difficulty in mentoring and prefer a team of "yes-men".

While I am not a psychiatrist, I do suspect that I have had colleagues that show high up on the spectrum of this personality disorder. One fellow director would often approach my team and demand an action which I had not approved or put in their priority lists. When they refused he would first resort to aggression and bullying, and if that did not succeed he would try to charm them. It never occurred to him to try and persuade me that the work-stream warranted taking priority over others and therefore being prioritised! The same director seemed to believe he had the right to challenge any of his colleagues' output, with or without data, but would be excessively aggressive and defensive if any critique was directed at his own. I never knew him to admit fault or show any conscience for his behaviours. Do you recognise colleagues or leaders in your organisation with the same traits? Do you recognise world leaders that you might suspect of being narcissistic?

Anti social personality disorder includes both sociopaths and at the most extreme psychopaths. NB These two should not be confused. Psychopathy can be thought of as a more severe form of sociopathy with more symptoms, often leading to criminal behaviour. All psychopaths are sociopaths but sociopaths are not necessarily psychopaths!

Sociopath behavioural traits include the following:

- o   Not necessarily violent but seek to dominate.
- o   Don't care much about the feelings of others.
- o   Easily frustrated, get aggressive, and quick to display anger.
- o   Dishonest; pervasive lying and deception.
- o   Simultaneously charm and humiliate to get what they want.
- o   Impulsive, with disregard for the safety of self or others.
- o   Lack of guilt or remorse and little concern for consequences; see nothing wrong with their behaviour.

Again, there are colleagues that I can remember who displayed behaviours of this type. Anecdotally, one manager visited the director of a supplier at his home and threatened to beat him up unless he guaranteed a better quality of fresh product! Can you think of colleagues that fit this mould? Even psychiatrists admit these behaviours are just extreme exaggerations of what is socially prevalent and that is what makes sociopaths so hard to identify and diagnose.

SYNOPSIS OF SECTION ONE

I have demonstrated that there are some highly suspect behaviours within our work places. Behaviours that are beyond the social norms of acceptance and are insidious by nature. Behaviours which in isolation may seem trivial but betray mindsets that are poorly motivated, and in their repetitive nature inflict countless injuries on morale. Behaviours that steamroll over our Social Contracts with each other and stretch the Work Contracts beyond satisfaction. Behaviours which, in the main, do not attract censure or consequences.

I believe these behaviours to be prevalent in many organisations and at all levels of each hierarchy. The behaviours are displayed by even those amongst us who are supposed to be positive role models and are trusted to lead our organisations.

I have called the people who behave in this way the Casual Leaders. Casual in their mindsets; casual in their behaviours; casual in approach to their responsibilities; and casual in the damage they cause to people's self-esteem, feelings of safety and collective goal.

BEWARE THE CASUAL LEADERS –
THEY LEAVE CASUALTIES WHEREVER THEY GO

- They DEMAND respect for their position because they cannot COMMAND respect for their qualities or their abilities (or both!).
- They assume SUPERIORITY rather than AUTHORITY and act with ENTITLEMENT.
- They are meant to be positive role models but do not set exemplary standards of behaviour. Rather than leaders by example they are MISLEADERS and NEGATIVE ROLE MODELS if we were to follow their conduct.
- Rather than lead from the front, THEY LEAD PEOPLE ASTRAY.

These Casual Leaders damage the morale of the organisations they are entrusted with and they destroy the most important commodity for any organisation – trust.

We have examined some of the potential causes of this behaviour. A lack of social perspective. An underdeveloped self-awareness. Misplaced ego and assumption of superiority. The power of their own role models on unconscious thought processes and behaviours. A personality disorder. But who is at fault?

How do Casual Leaders get into our organisations? How do Casual Leaders get promoted to positions of status and power? Why are Casual Leaders trusted with managing people, their contribution and their potential? Why do Casual Leaders' behaviours and actions not attract censure and consequences? *How do they get away with it?*

THE ACCOUNTABILITY OF THE CEO

"THE TROUBLE WITH YOU, ANDY, IS THAT YOU ARE TOO KIND TO YOUR TEAM AND TOO HARD ON YOUR BOSS"

It was an insightful critique from a man who was widely respected in the industry and who had forged a highly acclaimed career within the top company. He and I had been commercial partners for seven productive and highly successful years creating innovative concepts that were seen as market-leading. I saw him as a mentor and greatly admired his shrewd insight.

And it made me think! Was I too compassionate with my team? Did I have too much empathy? Possibly. I have a highly people-centric idea of management. I believe everyone has the right to be treated in the right way, be trained and developed, and be encouraged to stretch themselves beyond their comfort zones. I believe everyone has the right to develop their potential to feel accomplishment and to have the best possible career. But I was probably too nurturing at times also, in part as I felt I had to compensate for the impact of others.

And was I too hard on the boss? Too critical and intolerant? Set too high a bar of behaviour to expect of them? Well, not in this instance. For me, mine was only a mild criticism and my colleague should have heard what I had to say about other bosses in previous companies. In fact, the company was particularly well led in my experience and I felt valued and respected, allowing me to achieve.

Simon Sinek argues that people are increasingly reduced to abstracts in a world that is obsessed with metrics. He was talking about a lack of empathy and tolerance as we obsess about sales, profit, costs, productivity, return on investment etc. He argues that this abstraction creates distance from the people employed, which corrupts the sense of responsibility that leaders have towards others. "There is a lack of empathy and humanity in the way we do business today."

And I would agree. We even hide behind collective nouns and lose the identity of individuals. We talk about the staff, the leadership, the management, the directors, the board etc. and forget that these are made up of individuals. Different people, different personalities, different motivations, different needs and different styles.

Both metrics and collective nouns dehumanise the individual transactions and exchanges that collectively drive the achievements of any organisation. As Norman Schwarzkopf, retired US Army general and leader of the coalition forces in the first Gulf War, once said:

I have seen competent leaders who stood in front of a platoon and all they saw was a platoon. But great leaders stand in front of a platoon and see it as forty-four individuals, each of whom has aspirations, each of whom wants to live, each of whom wants to do good.

But there is one position in an organisation that is never a collective noun. And by and large s/he is the person most driven by the metrics – the CEO.

WHAT SHOULD A CEO DO?

Most people would concede that the CEO is a unique position in any organisation. As Drucker said in 2004, "The CEO is the link between the Inside that is the organisation, and the Outside of society, technology, markets, and customers."

The managing director/chief executive is the most senior full-time employee of the company. Many CEOs interpret the main purpose of their job as being to direct and control the company's operations; and to give strategic guidance and direction to ensure the company achieves its purpose and objectives. In practice that means the CEO has to balance the short term via the allocation of resources to most cost-effectively deliver current performance, and the long term through the investment of resources required to deliver sustainability.

They give an enormous amount of their time to:

o proposing the strategy;
o preparing the annual plan;
o monitoring its progress throughout the year to make it cost-efficient and effective.

They involve themselves in:

o   product/offer/service innovation;
o   reducing costs;
o   maximising revenue;
o   supplier negotiations;
o   the public image of the company;
o   competitor benchmarking;
o   quality management;
o   health and safety;
o   legal compliance;
o   monitoring service levels; and
o   preparation of the annual report.

All of which is essential and very important. Most of which is reported on at least monthly, some weekly, and, in the case of sales, daily or even hourly. There are metric reports galore, with exhaustive detail, and sometimes so frequent that agreed actions to address performance have not yet taken place.

BUT WHAT SHOULD A CEO BE DOING AS WELL?

Most developed countries in the world have a set of rules to cover corporate governance. Many of these refer to three influential reports published since 1990: the Cadbury Report (UK, 1992); the Principles of Corporate Governance (Organisation for Economic Co-operation and Development, 1999, 2004, 2005); and the Sarbanes–Oxley Act (USA, 2002). These rules set out the best practice for listed companies and large private companies are encouraged to abide by them. The main principles that they cover are:

o   The rights and equitable treatment of shareholders;
o   The interests of other stakeholders;

- Disclosure and financial transparency;
- Integrity and ethical behaviour;
- The role and responsibilities of the board.

The UK was ranked as the country with the highest rating for corporate governance in the world in 2010 (GMI Ratings, Sept 2010). Here the roles of chairman, CEO and other members of the board are prescribed under the UK Corporate Governance Code. This Code is published by the Financial Reporting Council (FRC) and its directors are appointed by the Secretary of State for Business, Energy and Industrial Strategy. Many UK regulators publish an additional specific code to reflect their own sector sensitivies (e.g. the Bank of England through the Prudential Regulation Authority for Banks, Building Societies and Insurers). But all of this is subject to the UK Corporate Governance Code and related legislation, e.g. the Companies Act 2006.

In my experience, few CEOs seem to prioritise Point 71 in the FRC Guidance on Board Effectiveness (2018):

71. The Chief Executive has primary responsibility for setting an example to the company's workforce, for communicating to them the expectations in respect of the company's culture, and for ensuring that operational policies and practices drive appropriate behaviour.

For the FRC, the CEO has a primary responsibility to be a positive role model for appropriate behaviours. In fact the FRC take values and the resultant culture very seriously indeed. Of the sixty points on "Guidance for an Effective Board", culture is referenced in nine points and values in eight points. They are the most permeating theme in the guidance, even more so than company purpose or long-term sustainability of the company!

In practice, CEOs are not alone in ignoring this guidance. An influential networking group for directors, who arrange training for CEOs too, published a leaflet entitled "The Main Responsibilities of the Managing Director" (31 May 2017). This leaflet makes no reference to culture or values at all, although it does recommend "the recruitment and retention of... well motivated, trained and developed staff."

Of course not all CEOs ignore or pay lip service to their critical role in being a positive role model and ensuring appropriate behaviours. In his *Harvard Business Review* article, "What Only the CEO Can Do" (May 2009), A.G. Lafley detailed four critical functions of the CEO. As former CEO of Proctor & Gamble, he listed shaping the values and standards of the organisation as one of those critical roles of the CEO.

> *We believe that P&G people are the company's most valuable assets. Without them we would have no P&G brands, no P&G innovation, and no P&G partnerships... Values establish a company's identity; they're about behaviour... In the absence of explicitly defined standards, people will develop their own; that's human nature.*

Lafley knew the top 500 people in the organisation and was involved personally in career planning the 150 who were earmarked for succession plans.

> *Little if anything else I do as CEO will have as enduring an impact on P&G's long-term future.*

And many commentators agree. Steve Radcliffe writes:

> *Being clear on just the vision, the strategy and the structure is never enough. We've found a clear statement of the culture or desired behaviours of ways of working is essential... Each*

of the team will then need to be seen as a walking example of this culture.

In his article "The Five Critical Roles of a CEO" (Aug, 2016), Terry Irwin of TCii Strategic and Management Consultants says:

> *A values-driven culture is key to high performance. CEOs ignore this at their peril. The CEO must build the culture he or she wants by consistently applying the organisation's values. Employees begin to notice when certain rules only apply to certain individuals or departments.*

Maybe my colleague was right in his critique that I was "hard on the boss". But I am not the only one who expects exemplary conduct from the boss and for them to set an example to the rest of us.

> *"Without strategy, execution is aimless. Without execution, strategy is useless." – Morris Chang, the founder, former chairman and CEO of TSMC, and known as the semiconductor industry founder of Taiwan.*

For me, the role of the CEO is to get results and that is all about the people in the organisation. Without people there is no one to tell the purpose of the organisation, to engage on the vision, and no one to do the work! It is about maximising the potential of the current workforce by determining the right behaviours to deliver a healthy culture. It is about choosing the right leaders at every level of the organisation and putting in the right incentives and consequences. It is about recruiting the right people and then training and developing them. It is about creating a culture of trust in which all layers of the organisation have a common goal; where co-operation, communication and teamwork can thrive; where accountability is clear and reward matches achievement; where training, development and coaching are encouraged; where policies, processes and decision-making are objective and efficient; where it is safe to raise concerns and voice opinions. And it is about being stringent with people who do not or will not behave in the right way, exiting them from the organisation if necessary.

> *"The growth and development of people is the highest calling of leadership."* – *Harvey S. Firestone, founder of one of the first global makers of car tyres and one of the largest companies in the industry.*

All of this is down to the CEO. They set the standards, and the standards they accept become the norm. If they ignore the Social Contract, others will follow their lead. If they consistently feel entitled to abuse the Work Contract, others will demand it of their own people. If they are not the positive role model for the organisation they are not doing their job. If they do not ensure meeting both the Social and Work Contracts, they are failing in their primary duty as CEO. If they are not creating a culture of trust and teamwork, they are guilty of evading their responsibilities.

So what else should a CEO be doing?

1 Making sure that people matter; ensuring s/he has the right people and that they are managed well.
2 Setting the values for the organisation and being the example of them in action.
3 Ensuring the desired culture is communicated and delivered through the behaviours, processes and procedures.

WHO WANTS TO BE A CEO?

No one should be more visible than the CEO. In the past, I have known CEOs to be all but invisible within an organisation, but that is increasingly not the case. With the advent of Skype, video meetings, conference calls, blogs, newsletters, intranet videos etc. augmenting the infrequent conferences of yesteryear, the CEO is usually highly visible in an organisation, at least to the management teams. And most CEOs take communication of their vision highly seriously so they embrace all opportunities to tell people.

No one is more observed than the CEO. No one is more listened to. No one has their actions and behaviour more dissected and critiqued.

And the vast majority of employees start with goodwill. They want to respect the CEO. They want to look up to the CEO both as a person – for their qualities and their strength of character – and for their competence – for their abilities and certainty of decision-making. I believe a lot of CEOs take this for granted as if their status demands this blessing of goodwill by right.

As we explored previously, I don't subscribe to the Dilbert Principle. Nor have I found the Peter Principle to be true of

CEOs themselves. Both principles would suggest that the CEO is the ultimate resting place of incompetence as the vast majority have had to learn the role on the job, never having done it before. Edward Lazeer suggested in 2000 that there were two other phenomena that developed the thinking behind the Peter Principle: (1) that employees work hard to get a promotion, and then slack off once it is achieved; (2) employees get promoted after achieving a level of productivity based on factors that cannot be replicated in the new role. He determined that the former only happens with certain reward structures but the latter always holds true! And if either phenomena were true you would surely find that of a CEO. After all, they have reached the pinnacle of the hierarchy with nowhere else to go in that organisation; many have never had the job before and they do reap the benefits of a unique reward package. But that is not my experience of CEOs. Care has been taken in their selection and by and large they are competent to make decisions. Their knowledge, skills and experience will have been exhaustively examined. The following criteria will have been met:

o   A proven track record of success and progression
o   Experience in managing people and resource
o   Qualifications indicating a degree of intellect
o   Understanding of financial management, legislative requirements and other management principles
o   A high level of commercial awareness
o   Good communication and organisational skills
o   Good analytical and problem-solving skills.

However, it is of course a fallacy that the CEO is the best businessperson. And that should not surprise us. A head teacher is not necessarily the best tutor; a general is not going to be the best marksman. The skill sets for a great CEO as a general manager are different from those that make a good specialist manager or director. I know of many people who were highly capable businesspeople, and possibly more competent than their CEO, but who never aspired to be the CEO. They may not have had the ambition; they may not have had the drive; they may have preferred a role with better work–life balance; they may have resolved that they had sufficient earnings to live the life they wanted; or they may just not have been confident enough. So what is it that drives someone to become a CEO, and does that make them the ultimate positive role model?

The work of social psychologist and cross-cultural researcher Shalom Schwartz may help our understanding. Professor Schwartz is president of the International Association for Cross-Cultural Psychology and a fellow of the American Psychological Foundation. In the 1970s and 1980s his work was pioneering in understanding cross-cultural behaviour. Unhelpfully he calls his work "The Theory of Basic Human Values", which is not the same definition of values I have been using. Instead of our initial definition as "the basic rules of how to live in reasonable harmony with other people", Schwartz's definition of values is the motivational drivers that act as guiding principles for one's life.

Schwartz has identified ten such drivers of behaviour following a survey of over 60,000 people in over eighty countries. These include:

1   Hedonism – to seek pleasure and sensual gratification for oneself above all things.
2   Stimulation – novelty, challenge, excitement and thrills from experiences.
3   Universalism – social justice, protection and tolerance; looking after your social group and nature.
4   Benevolence – seeking to help others; looking after and enhancing the welfare of your social group.

5 Tradition – respecting, accepting and committing to customs; following traditions and norms of a social group or religion.

6 Conformity – obedience to clear rules and structures; restraint of one's own inclinations, impulses and actions that violate social norms or might lead to harm of others.

7 Security – seeking health and safety; harmony and stability of self, relationships and social groups.

8 Self-direction – independence of thought and action, particularly artistically or creatively.

But the most likely to drive the ambition to become a CEO, in my opinion, are either:

9 Power – the ability to control other people and resources. To seek dominance. Importance is put on social status and prestige.

10 Achievement – setting goals and achieving them. The greater the challenge, the greater the sense of achievement. When others achieve the same, higher goals are set. Personal success is felt through demonstrating greater-than-average competence.

Schwartz continues to develop his theory in collaboration with others, as shown by a follow-up paper in 2012. He believes that none of these universal motivations is exclusive and we can be driven by a combination of motivations. However, it is clear also that some of them are selfish and centred entirely on gratifying our own desires while others are selfless and subordinate our own needs for the benefit of a wider social group. A good CEO would need to balance at least some of their selfish drivers with others that have a greater bearing on the welfare of their organisation.

SELFLESS MOTIVATIONS Orientated to benefit a social group	SELFISH MOTIVATIONS Orientated to gratifying oneself
Universalism	Hedonism
Benevolence	Stimulation
Tradition	Self-direction
Conformity	Power
Security	Achievement

Clearly, if the main driver or motivation for a CEO is power, rather than achievement, then their leadership style will be fairly definite and they are unlikely to be a good role model! If power is the major driver, then setting and living the best behaviour or values of a culture is going to be impaired. Their ego-state is much more inclined to that of "critical parent" than either "nurturing parent" or "adult". People are unlikely to matter to them, and there is little chance that either the Social Contract or Work Contract will be respected. Nor is there much likelihood of the CEO being respected, in turn, for their personal qualities. They are more likely to be feared.

> "You can fool all of the people some of the time, and some of the people all of the time, but you cannot fool all of the people all of the time." – Abraham Lincoln

Employees soon get a measure of what type of person is their CEO. They may not be able to articulate it but they do know if they respect them as a person and whether they trust them. Of course some CEOs make it easy to judge who they are from what they say or do, but it may not even take that.

Professor Albert Mehrabian has pioneered the understanding of communications since the 1960s. Currently he is professor emeritus of psychology, UCLA, and has become best known by his publications on the relative importance of verbal and nonverbal messages. These were derived from experiments dealing with communications of feelings and attitudes (i.e. like–dislike). He devised the classic statistic for understanding the effectiveness of spoken communication and in particular the meaning behind spoken words:

o   7% of meaning is in the words used;
o   38% of meaning is in the tone of voice;
o   55% of meaning is in the body language and particularly facial expression.

So if power is the CEO's motivation, and "critical parent" is their ego-state, they could be showing it every time they are observed or heard. This is not about their words; their tone of voice and body language will show if they believe what they say or if they are authentic and trustworthy. It is not beyond possible that they may show the manipulation, selfishness or paranoia of the narcissist or the dishonesty, lack of guilt and supreme indifference to others of the sociopath. They may get short-term results that encourage them but in the long term this will not succeed and they will fail to build the potential of their employees. These CEOs are unlikely to be positive role models or be trusted by their teams. People will not matter. Values will be erratic. Culture will be chaotic.

If achievement is the CEOs motivation, and "adult" is their ego-state, their communication of attitude and feelings are positioned well to recruit followers and be the positive role model their employees deserve and will trust. It will be clear that people matter, the values will be modelled by the CEO and there will be a clear expectation of the right culture.

WHAT EXAMPLE SHOULD A CEO SET?

One company I worked for was fond of saying, "What gets measured gets done." In researching for this book I found the original quote which is far more powerful. It was of course from Peter Drucker but he said, "What gets measured gets improved."

But what metrics are there for people, values and culture? In my experience, while there are metrics galore for everything else, there are few if any for leading by example, policing behaviour, or measuring progress on culture. In fact, while I would have spent hours every week, and days every month, going over key commercial metrics with my own boss, years would go by without any meaningful discussion on my management style, my profile within the business, or about my people.

What "people" measures there are seem primarily about managing costs: monitoring payroll, reducing absenteeism, filling vacancies or policing expenses. I would be asked often to justify my headcount but would never be faced with a report on what training and development my team warranted or had taken part in. I got asked rarely on my succession planning but never what coaching or mentoring I had done. Two teams I inherited had had no training of any kind in the four years before I took responsibility for them! The budget was non-existent, having been cut to meet profit targets years before.

The only report that even came close to measuring aspects of culture and placing importance on people and values was the staff engagement survey, and it only happened annually.

As part of its corporate governance guide, the FRC recommends that engagement surveys are undertaken and most companies I worked for did commission them. However, in practice they are a blunt tool and open to wide interpretation. The vast majority of the questions concentrate on: understanding the company's purpose, the frequency and quality of the communication cascade, and perceptions of the company as a whole. For me, they often fail to be specific about individuals and the causes of disengagement.

I have found also that these surveys are open to abuse but largely ignored in any case. Abuse? Yes. No matter how anonymous they are supposed to be, it is usually possible to identify the author of low scores or anyone who is likely to be critical in a particular sphere of questions. I have known directors actively hunt down dissenters within their poll in the past. Over the years, that led to artificially high scores for engagement in their teams as people were terrified of being identified as being critical. Another technique I have seen employed is directors ensuring full payment of bonuses to those that showed engagement in their results. But, in any case, it seemed to me to be largely a tick-box exercise. Something to boast about if scores improved and shrugged off if they declined. I cannot remember any meaningful debate or analysis at board level, or any interrogation of the meaning of the results by my boss – ever. Over the years, this has led to lower completion rates and greater cynicism from employees. Even if subsequent action was taken and communicated, I found employees failed to give credibility or credence to the survey, or recognise that efforts had been made to address criticism.

FOR ME, THE FIRST THING THAT A CEO SHOULD SET AN EXAMPLE OF IS THAT PEOPLE MATTER

I have attended endless annual conferences where people have never been presented or discussed. (One company never even discussed consumers or competitors either!) I have had personal appraisals where neither my leadership strengths and weaknesses nor my people have been discussed. When I worked for a global company, I would have quarterly business reviews with group board members and never were the quality, capability, training or aspiration of my people discussed. In my whole career, I have only attended one "round table" with a CEO to discuss the individuals of the company leadership team across departments. I cannot remember more than a handful of monthly operating boards where people have been discussed. For years, in my monthly one-to-ones with CEOs or directors, people were only discussed if I raised the subject. Any discussion on succession planning or training has been scarcer than the dodo!

When CEOs are genuinely committed to people and engagement they are addressing this equation:

ENGAGEMENT = REWARD MINUS SACRIFICE

Here, "reward" is so much more than just pay, bonuses, pension, health care, employee discounts, holidays etc., which are all held in the Work Contract.

Reward includes also: clarity of purpose and role; status; influence; autonomy; accuracy of feedback; recognition; respect; acknowledgement; mental stimulation; challenge; support; learning; development; achievement; trust. These are all delivered with leadership skills that come from a position of empathy and need to be addressed.

And "sacrifice" includes more than just time. It also includes: self-respect; dignity; work–life balance; physical effort; emotional and spiritual diminishment. Most of these exist within the Social Contract and need to be recognised.

The moment that sacrifice outweighs reward, there is a problem. And so the CEO should set an example that people matter by starting to measure, report and discuss all the other elements that don't appear in a cost line to be managed.

A good starting place is to appoint a dedicated HR director to his board with a remit that is wider than "people issues" and so includes effective leadership selection and monitoring of culture. Many boards don't even have an HR director – what signal does that give that people matter? Then the CEO should ensure that time is scheduled to discuss people and culture in each of his board meetings and in each of his meetings with his own direct reports. And then the CEO should stop viewing training and development budgets as a cost line to be reduced, but start seeing it as an investment in the organisation's future that needs to be optimised. But we will discuss the mechanics, policies and processes that ensure people matter later on in the book. For now the CEO just has to show people matter in what he says and does – in his leadership style.

THE NEXT THING A CEO HAS TO DO IS DETERMINE THE RIGHT VALUES AND BE A LIVING EXAMPLE OF THEM

Later on we will talk through how to determine the specific values for an individual organisation. These are most likely to be weighted toward teamwork and task completion by many organisations, but should not be exclusively so. For now, though, it should be taken as read that the CEO must set an example of the values held in both the Social Contract and also the Work Contract at the bare minimum. If they do not uphold either of these contracts they cannot be seen as believing people matter. If they hold others to these standards, but not themselves, they are seen as hypocrites and will never secure trust or respect.

"Do as I say, not as I do" will never secure the hearts and minds of employees. Conversely they will respect you if you live by these standards and hold others to them – and one value in particular is critical to building trust.

THE THIRD THING A CEO SHOULD SET AS AN EXAMPLE TO THE REST OF THE ORGANISATION IS HOW TO MAKE DECISIONS

The CEO is not a specialist any more. They may have risen through the hierarchy of one particular discipline or even held a position as director in another discipline, but they are now a general manager. Their previous experience and skill set as an accountant (for example) still has some relevance but they are now in charge of seasoned, specialist directors for each discipline. People who have had hard-won years of experience in their disciplines, which cannot be subsumed by a more senior title.

The great CEOs recognise that they do not have those years of dedication in each discipline. They know they may have the final and eventual decision but they are not best placed to propose every solution. An accountant who has become a CEO has never briefed a creative agency for an advertising film. A purchasing director who has become a CEO has never designed a retail experience or briefed designers and building companies. An operator who has become a CEO has never designed a new product or liaised with factory managers on efficiency of production methods. Nor are their spouses or children a great source of insight either. Most marketing and purchasing directors will have heard feedback from the CEO that starts with, "My wife/partner thinks...". A friend of mine is constantly being given the critique of the CEO's seventeen-year-old daughter on his latest promotion or PR release as she studies for her HND in communication studies. If only the

CEOs understood the damage they do to their own reputation and respect when they validate the views of family members as better than twenty or thirty years' worth of specialist experience as well as the access to all the market metrics and latest analysis.

The great CEOs have the humility to understand that they do have experts and specialists whose whole careers have led them to the point of leading the entire discipline for that company. The CEO should not have to read every piece of consumer analysis, every data set, every research report, or need to remember and balance every nuance of legislation. The great CEO doesn't need to do any of that because he knows he is paying for a specialist to do that!

Again, the FRC has captured this point in its Guidance on Board Effectiveness.

> 16. *The boardroom should be a place for robust debate where challenge, support, diversity of thought and teamwork are essential features. Diversity of skills, background and personal strengths is an important driver of a board's effectiveness, creating different perspectives amongst directors, and breaking down a tendency toward "group think".*

What the CEO does have to do is to ensure rigorous debate and examine the robustness of the thinking. A great CEO ensures that the work of each discipline is joined up to make a cohesive thought process and an action plan that can proceed at pace and cost-effectively. Just because the CEO has the final say does not mean they should delude themselves that they have suddenly become superior decision makers in every discipline they have no experience in.

And yet so many do. Perhaps it is because power is their motivation, or perhaps because power does indeed corrupt, but I have seen the rush of blood that goes to the head of some

CEOs. For one reason or another, some CEOs decide not only do they need to make the final decision but they have to propose every solution also, plus its architecture and priority.

Frequently this seems to be based on the CEO's intuition or on giving preference to only one trusted source of information. I do believe there is scope for intuition in business but it has to be recognised for what it is, and then ruthlessly tested by securing data and facts to prove or disprove it. Intuition is only a working hypothesis, after all. And if it cannot be backed up by investigation and testing, it is only an unproven hypothesis – what marketers call self-reference criteria – "I think therefore it is true". Rightly, no CEO would accept an intuitive argument from anyone else in the business that is not fully supported by analysis, but so many CEOs seem to ignore this stringent test of their own thinking. And these CEOs are the hardest to influence, as once they have set out their stall they cannot bear to be seen to be changing their mind, as if it is shameful not to have thought of everything or to admit a mistake. And so companies knowingly do the wrong thing or set out actions in a less effective order as the ego of the CEO prevents adjusting the plan.

In his book *Winning*, Jack Welch said that, to get the bigger and better solutions, leaders had to probe proposals by asking questions and stimulating debate. "You have to be incredibly comfortable looking like the dumbest person in the room. Every conversation you have about a decision, a proposal or piece of market information has to be filled with you saying 'What if?' and 'Why not?' and 'How come?'"

For me, the CEO should be setting the example of how to ensure full consultation and debate prior to making the decision. The CEO should listen first and speak last. The CEO has to stimulate the debate through open questions, challenging and exploring the thinking; the CEO needs to draw out other views and information from within the debate; the CEO needs to ensure that all have contributed and felt consulted in the process; and finally the CEO needs to support and build on the proposals with these other perspectives, and from their own experience, to get to the best solution.

The CEO should be demonstrating through their own conduct that: people matter, there is a right way to behave, and the culture should be respectful and collaborative. If the CEO were a positive example to the rest of the organisation on just these three things then they would be well on the way to creating an engaged workforce that can perform at the highest level.

WHAT LEADERSHIP STYLE IS THE MOST EFFECTIVE?

A CEO probably needs more than one style. In fact, research suggests that a good CEO needs to be a chameleon to enhance their effectiveness, and should be able to adopt different styles according to the needs of any given situation and for different audiences. I would suggest however that one style would be most natural for any individual and that would be the dominant one in forming the culture around a CEO.

Daniel Goleman is an internationally known psychologist and recognised as an expert in emotional intelligence. In 2000, he published an article called "Leadership That Gets Results" in the *Harvard Business Review*. This was followed up by the book *Primal Leadership*, which he wrote in collaboration with Richard Boyatzis and Annie McKee.

Goleman's work is based on interviews with nearly 4,000 executives, from which he identified six leadership styles. He argues that a good executive should master these styles, see them as a strategic choice rather than a necessity born from personality, and deploy different styles depending on the circumstances. However, to be able to do so, the most successful leaders have to have strengths in four emotional capabilities (which have twenty underlying competencies):

o **Self-awareness:** an honest and realistic evaluation of your own strengths and weaknesses; the ability to understand your own emotions and their impact on your own performance and that of others; a strong and positive sense of self-worth.

o **Self-management:** control over your own emotions and impulses; the ability to adjust to changing circumstance; a drive to achieve an internal standard of excellence; conscientiousness and a readiness to seize opportunities, allied to a consistent set of behaviours that create trustworthiness.

o **Social awareness:** empathetic skill at understanding others' emotions and perspectives and addressing their concerns; organisational sensitivity and the ability to build networks; and a service orientation to recognise and meet customer needs.

o **Social skill:** the ability to inspire, influence and develop others; skill at defusing conflicts, building relationships and promoting co-operation and teamwork; highly developed communication skills and a proficiency to initiate new ideas.

Goleman's analysis showed that one leadership style was clearly the most positive on the culture of an organisation – the Authoritative Style (sometimes called the Visionary Style). This style mobilises people with an inspiring vision and says "Come with me". This leader "motivates people by making clear to them how their work fits into a larger vision of the organisation". S/he tells the team where they are all going but not how they're going to get there, instead leaving it up to team members to find the right solutions to meet the vision. This style enhances the sense of accuracy on personal feedback and therefore the fairness of rewards; it gives clarity of purpose and builds commitment to a common goal; and encourages ownership and innovation by employees. The only drawback of this style is that it can be less effective when the leader is working with a team of experts who are more experienced than s/he is.

Please do NOT confuse "authoritative" with "authoritarian"! An "authoritative" leadership style is where compliance is commanded because of the leader's self-confidence, respect, trust, honesty, accuracy and reliability; it allows personal freedom. On the other hand, an authoritarian leader enforces strict obedience to authority by restricting any personal freedom and behaving in an autocratic way like a tyrant or despot.

I believe that leaders that employ the authoritative style most frequently must have achievement as their motivation and be in an adult ego-state.

Good Leaders who have the authoritative style will also use other styles at times to enhance their impact. Goleman identified three other positive styles:

1 **Affiliative Style**, where people come first and they feel valued. Particularly useful in healing rifts in teams or getting through crises but its exclusive focus on optimism and praise can allow poor performance not to be addressed.
2 **Democratic Style**, which forges consensus through broad participation – "What do you think?" This helps buy-in but delays decision-making; it can lead to endless committees and meetings, leaving people confused and leaderless.
3 **Coaching Style** or "Try this". This style develops individuals by improving performance and developing their potential.

It seems to me that these styles are also motivated by an achievement driver, but may show a nurturing parent ego-state.

Two of the leadership styles identified by Goleman should only be used sparingly. They have a purpose for specific challenges but over time are highly damaging to the culture of the organisation:

1 **The Coercive Style or "Do what I tell you"**

This style can be appropriate in times of crisis, to kick-start a turnaround or to shock a problem employee, as it demands immediate compliance. But Goleman identifies this leadership style as the least effective of them all in most situations. "If a leader relies solely on this style or continues to use it once the emergency passes, the long-term impact of his insensitivity to the morale and feelings of those he leads will be ruinous."

This leadership style destroys innovation as people feel disrespected and that their suggestions will be ignored. Personal responsibility evaporates and people lose the sense of accountability for their performance. Pride is lost in doing tasks well so the job is less rewarding and motivation is destroyed. In fact this style is negative on most measurements of a healthy culture and only has a marginal positive effect on the standards that people set.

Perhaps the achievement of dominance and power from this leadership style is triggering a rush of adrenaline for the CEO? Perhaps this is compensating for a long-held feeling of inadequacy or is a response to high challenge and stress on themselves? As we will see later, that can spill over into outright aggression. However, whichever way you look at, if this style is used predominantly, it does not enable employees. Instead it disables their motivation and potential.

I know of one company that was led like this and the CEO even had a unique phrase that entered the company lexicon – JFDI (Just F***ing Do It). If ever an organisation had given up on engaging their people in a vision, it was this one. Christopher's own board would ask him not to attend strategy brainstorming meetings as they felt intimidated by him. And when one business unit tried to address the culture with a programme entitled "Our People, Our Future", the business was littered with Post-it notes the next day saying "Our People, No Future" or "Our People, What Future?".

But at least that CEO worked hard to understand the market and the business in an effort to drive results. I know of another CEO with this style who had no experience of the market and coerced his highly experienced team into numerous poor initiatives that distracted from the day-to-day actions that would drive results. There was never any consultation, dissent was met with anger and people's workloads increased exponentially. During Shaun's induction period he had listed the operating board's maturity, stability and experience as one of the strengths of the organisation. Within eighteen months, five of the seven-person-strong team had left.

I know of another CEO who was so driven for results that he would annually unveil the twenty-one global priorities and then expect local markets to add a further ten initiatives of their own. Again, workloads increased exponentially, initiatives were delivered badly, morale sank like a stone and results stayed stagnant as there was no focus.

2   The Pacesetting Style or "Do as I do, now"
This style focusses on performance and meeting goals. These leaders expect excellence from their teams and exemplify these standards themselves; often the leader jumps in to make sure that goals are met. S/he is obsessive about things going better and faster, and s/he asks the same of everyone else. S/he quickly pinpoints poor performers and demands more from them.

You would think this style would be effective but it destroys the organisation's culture. People are overwhelmed by the demands on them, and work becomes a matter of second-guessing what the leader wants. Morale drops as people feel they are not trusted to take the initiative; responsibility and commitment evaporate; and work becomes so task-focussed it becomes tedious. This leadership style damages the standards that people set and confuses the clarity of purpose employees have for the mission and the appropriate behaviours. The only time this approach works well is if employees are self-motivated, highly competent and need little co-ordination, e.g. a legal team.

Are these CEOs hooked on the adrenaline triggered by the excitement of the pace they set? Or perhaps they are experiencing the chemical rush of dopamine, triggered by getting things done, or from endorphins, which are the "runner's high", to compensate for the extremes they are asking of themselves? Are these chemicals making this behaviour a compulsive way of working to get their "fix"?

One CEO that used this style predominantly, but alternated with the coercive style of leadership too, ended up micromanaging everything. Intelligent, hard-working and passionate about detail but with no empathy for customers or concern for his staff, Neil's fingers were in every pie. Eventually he was surrounded by a team of "yes-men" who acquiesced to whatever he wanted, which was primarily driven by his own view of the world. His operational director had been widely respected for his drive and commercial erudition but ended up saying, "What the boss wants, the boss gets," even when he disagreed with the actions being taken. His head of pricing ended up just providing analysis and reports, instead of recommendations, as any actions were decided by the CEO. The head of innovation was reduced to a role as a project manager. His marketing director became disillusioned as the CEO insisted on making subjective decisions, without reference to customers, on all the elements of the marketing mix –

price, product, communications, store design etc. – but still blaming marketing for poor like-for-like sales performance.

This CEO's behaviours were masked by a mild demeanour and courteous manner but effectively removed all the empowerment and motivation of his team without understanding the consequences. It was a quiet arrogance and disrespect for others that underpinned his character. Meanwhile, Neil was so busy doing the job of his subordinates that he misjudged two external economic threats to the business, which cost the company dearly.

When either of the Coercive or Pacesetting leadership styles are employed most of the time, it indicates that the CEO is a person with little empathy for others. They are lacking in emotional intelligence of themselves and their reactions and/or social intelligence in their own interaction and impact with others. In my view, power is most likely to be the motivation of the CEO when these styles are employed, and they clearly indicate a critical parent ego-state. There is plenty of challenge but no support. If the CEO were either a narcissist or a sociopath themselves, the Coercive or the Pacesetting leadership styles would be their dominant way of behaving.

Seasoned business managers know intuitively, and from experience, that leadership styles that negatively impact on the culture of the organisation also impact on the ability to drive results. Low morale leads to poor performance. And this is backed up by research.

Goleman quotes the findings of David McClelland, a noted Harvard University psychologist. McClelland found a causal relationship between a critical mass of six or more emotional intelligence competencies and actual results. Leaders with this critical mass of competencies tended to outperform targets by between +15% and +20%, whilst those that did not have this critical mass underperformed by –20% on average.

And Goleman's findings were similar. "Leaders who used styles that positively affected climate [culture] had decidedly better financial results than those who did not. That is not to say that organisational climate is the only driver of performance. Economic conditions and competitive dynamics matter enormously. But our analysis strongly suggests that climate accounts for nearly a third of results."

GOLEMAN'S LEADERSHIP STYLES IN THE MATRIX

Of course, McLelland and Goleman are not the only commentators on leadership styles. Karl Albrecht is an American psychologist and executive management consultant. He has developed a theory of "social intelligence" based on the work by Professor Howard Gardner of Harvard University on "multiple intelligences". It appears to me that Albrecht's theory is influenced also by the works of Professor Mehrabian and Eric Berne.

In his book *Social Intelligence: The New Science of Success*, Albrecht proposes a simpler model of multiple intelligence than Gardner and analyses social intelligence in particular. He believes that social intelligence is essential for understanding contexts, knowing how to navigate within and between them, and knowing how best to behave so as to achieve your objective.

It is a skill that he believes can be learned and significant improvements can be made but it is essential to have an honest understanding of your own social skills, in particular:

o appreciating the context you are in and how that is affecting others' behaviour;
o awareness of your own presence and the signals you send to others by the way you behave;
o the extent to which others think you are being authentic and honest;
o the ability to express ideas clearly and effectively; this includes the ability for active listening and to give accurate feedback while explaining things simply and concisely;
o the ability to build connections and bond with others so that there is a mutual respect and willingness to co-operate.

To measure these social skills, Albrecht has defined twenty-five different behaviours along a spectrum. At one end of the spectrum are "toxic" behaviours which leave others feeling devalued, inadequate, angry, frustrated or even feeling guilty. These are counterbalanced at the other end of the spectrum by "nourishing" behaviours which cause people to feel valued, capable, loved, respected and appreciated.

In my view, many of the toxic behaviours identified by Albrecht have all the hallmarks of the Coercive and/or the Pacesetting leadership styles identified by Goleman:

o Monopolising the conversation
o Ignoring or snubbing others
o Insisting on getting your own way
o Interrupting others, talking over them
o Shooting down others' ideas
o Disagreeing rudely or aggressively
o Expressing dogmatic or intolerant opinions

- Unfriendly demeanour, "keep away" signals
- Criticising, pushing unwanted advice
- Condescending, patronising, parenting others.

Some of the toxic behaviours cited by Albrecht I recognise in myself, e.g. joking inappropriately and overusing profanity! But it is the sheer number of behaviours and prevalence to behave in that way which severely impacts on the social intelligence of the individual. Each of the examples of CEOs that I suggested have Coercive or Pacesetting leadership styles would have scored badly on a significant number of the twenty-five behaviours.

It may seem paradoxical but I believe that CEOs that predominantly use the Coercive or Pacesetting styles are guilty of being Casual Leaders. They are certainly not casual in the approach to the task; if anything they are intimidating in their drive and focus. Many of them will believe that they are solely motivated by achievement and are simply task-orientated. They might argue passionately that they are in an adult ego-state, just very demanding and critical of the people around them. However, they must be underdeveloped emotionally and socially, having either no ability to control their own emotions and reactions and/or no social awareness of the context in which they are interacting with others and their own impact on them. Their disregard for everyone other than themselves is casual. Their behaviours are disrespectful, disempowering and intolerant. They are unaware that they destroy self-respect and morale, casually throwing away the commitment, energy, expertise and potential of their staff and of their teams.

If CEOs predominantly use the Coercive or Pacesetting leadership style, they are preparing a fertile ground for the growth of other Casual Leaders within the organisation. This is inevitable as they are showing a poor role model to follow and have poor social intelligence. And so, Casual Leaders at the top breed Casual Leaders throughout the hierarchy of management.

On the other hand, CEOs that are predominantly of the Authoritative leadership style do not tolerate Casual Leaders beneath them. Their positive role model provides an incentive to the managers beneath them, and they set consequences for any who display casual behaviours.

> "It doesn't make sense to hire smart people and tell them what to do; we hire smart people so they can tell us what to do." – Steve Jobs, co-founder of Apple Inc.

It seems to me that among the other criteria established for selecting a CEO, self-awareness and empathy are critical. Typically, the criteria currently used concentrate on abstract intelligence (conceptual reasoning; manipulating verbal, numeric and symbolic data) and practical intelligence (the ability to solve problems and get things done) with appropriate experience and knowledge. To this list should be added emotional intelligence (self-insight and the ability to control your own emotions and reactions) plus social intelligence (the ability to positively interact and influence others in a variety of contexts).

THEY NEED YOUR HELP

When I think back through my career, I can identify many weaknesses in the CEOs and managing directors I have observed. Below I have listed the most common:

o **Being Distant**
Distance can be taken for arrogance but will always prevent the CEO from being in touch with the real issues and shuts down debate.

o **People-Pleasing**
While courting popularity, this prevents abidance to values and takes the focus away from delivering results. Employees want strength of character, vision and drive from the CEO.

o **Coercive or Pacesetting Leadership Styles**
These two styles have a place in the CEO's repertoire – usually for a crisis – but must be used sparingly or they will cause more damage than good. Relying on these styles as the dominant tone for the organisation is foolhardy in the extreme even if it is an easy fit with their own personality.

Being too critical or not allowing ownership will only backfire in the long term.

∘ **Not Delivering Results**
All organisations need progress to lead to sustainability. Confidence from external stakeholders is key, but internal stakeholders and morale should not be sacrificed to achieve the required results.

∘ **Hypocrisy**
It is not enough to "talk the talk"; the CEO has to be a role model and set an example to the rest of the organisation by "walking the walk".

∘ **Personal Complacency**
The CEO lends energy and urgency to the organisation. And this includes the CEO pursuing continuous learning for themselves and others in this fast-paced, technological age where new skills and competencies are constantly required.

∘ **Being Overly Ambitious**
Challenges and targets need to stretch the organisation and individuals. But they also need to be realistic and confined to the resource available. Demanding increased productivity through an excessive quantity of time from the individual is lazy and irresponsible. Productivity will come from clarity and efficiency; once those are optimised, resource may need to be increased.

∘ **Not Taking Accountability for People**
To get the best from this resource, CEOs need to: ensure that people feel valued and recognised; invest in their potential through training and development; unleash their enthusiasm, drive and commitment by engaging them and

motivating them; give accurate feedback and reward them appropriately and fairly; remove Casual Leaders – they should not exist in the organisation and only below-average performers settle for poor leadership.

○ **Lacking Self-Awareness**
Emotional intelligence and social intelligence are essential to successfully lead people. It is the difference between "impact felt" and "impact intended", to quote Steve Radcliffe. The CEO's own personal credibility is essential and too many spend little time ensuring that they are aware of it, protecting it and developing it.

○ **Not Being Authentic**
People sniff out a phoney very quickly. Acting as if you know everything is never plausible. Nor is claiming to believe in something when your actions clearly indicate otherwise. And denying responsibility or ownership for a poor decision that you made fools no one. In all these examples the CEO comes across as dishonest and risks their entire credibility. If there is no humility, or no conviction, employees will soon determine that you are not trustworthy and then you will lose their passion and personal commitment. They simply will not believe in you or think you are credible. Genuine people are authentic – they are not infallible and they are not all-knowing; they do make mistakes. And everyone knows this.

○ **Not Addressing Inequities**
Many organisations nowadays are the result of mergers of different entities. This is due to consolidation to save costs and acquisitions to gain scale. As such, there are many "grandfather" rights preserved across organisations where different pay scales exist for the same job grade, or different entitlements exist for things such as holidays,

bonuses, health care or pension provision. Unless these are addressed, and brought into one cohesive structure and policy, the inequities are corrosive. CEOs cannot have one culture, aligned and pulling in the same direction, when rewards are disparate and unfair. Many CEOs fail to address these inequities as they require hard work and can mean increased cost. They fail to see that they cannot afford not to address them as they will never create an engaged culture until they do.

However, CEOs need our support too so that they can be the best version of themselves.

In 2017, Pricewaterhouse Coopers published their latest survey of CEOs worldwide. They evaluated the top 2,500 companies in the world and showed that CEOs' tenure is short and that a significant number of them had little experience.

Worldwide, the average tenure of a CEO is five years – in the UK it is even less at 4.8 years and has been decreasing for a number of years. The length of tenure gives little time for the CEO to make a significant impact on a company's performance and almost ensures that short-term interests will prevail. The annual turnover of roles was 16.3% in 2016, with more than 75% of new appointments going to candidates with no previous experience of leading a public company.

The CEO's job is a lonely one. Heading up the inside of an organisation and being its outside face gives plenty of challenge to the CEO. The CEO is not immune to this and, without support of their own, they will only feel anxiety and stress like the rest of us. Little prior experience does not help. S/he is exposed and vulnerable to the forceful self-interests of all the stakeholders, which will include the selfish, sycophants or manipulators inside or outside of the organisation. Without due care this could distort their perspective of themselves and the reality of the situation they are in.

The good CEOs are aware of this and ensure they have a powerful network to keep them grounded and aware of both themselves and the organisation. By necessity this network has to be external to be healthy or internal organisational relationships become distorted. If s/he chooses wisely this will include both people with understanding of the organisation and its marketplace for effectiveness, plus shrewd adult ego-state advisers for self-awareness and social empathy.

> *"If you ask any successful business person, they will always have had a great mentor at some point along the road." – Sir Richard Branson*

I do sympathise to an extent. "Uneasy lies the head that wears the crown," as Shakespeare wrote, but the CEO did volunteer for this role and does get the exceptional rewards that go with it, so buckle up and do the whole job, please.

For me, the CEO can also support themselves by critically evaluating and choosing the right team around them; and by creating the right culture in the organisation to foster their vision. If the board of directors is made up of Casual Leaders then the culture will never be engaged and high-performing! If the senior cadre of managers contains Casual Leaders they will create more beneath them and infect the whole organisation. Casual Leaders create Casual Leaders. It becomes a toxic spiral.

In the 1990s, the British anthropologist Robin Dunbar calculated that there is a maximum number of people that can be part of one fully functioning social group. Proponents suggest this is a range of between 100 and 250 people but it is commonly felt that the peak number is 150 people to comfortably sustain a social relationship. Clearly many companies far exceed that number and the CEO cannot be expected to influence all of these people alone. S/he has to be clear of expectations, delegate authority and then hold those leaders responsible for the effective management of subordinates. Most head office departments will be at a size where the director can execute that role and have frequent contact with the CEO, but in the case of retail or field sales the department size may be substantially larger. In those cases further layers of management (divisional, regional, area managers etc.) need to be entrusted with that responsibility and the CEO must create the right ways of working to ensure that they are: clear on expectations, performing on brief, visible in their actions and held to account. This cannot be delegated or managed with a low frequency method; the CEO must take personal responsibility and pull that layer of management into their own circle of 150 people to influence.

SYNOPSIS OF SECTION TWO

In this chapter, we have defined the role of the CEO and their accountability. They are the ULTIMATE ROLE MODEL for the organisation.

We have explored what they do and more importantly what they should do, but frequently do not. We have examined their motivations and recognised that they could be a Casual Leader as well.

At the end of the day, the CEO is accountable for results and these are always delivered by people.

The CEO has a duty to ensure that:

1   People are optimised as a resource and this comes from: showing that they matter, motivating them and developing their potential.
2   The right behaviours are set and that the CEO is the role model to the rest of the organisation on these. This includes how to run debates and how to make decisions.
3   The board is made up of directors that are also role models for the right behaviours and committed to developing the capability of the people who report into them. The CEO appoints or retains these people. S/he is accountable for their suitability in that role.

4   The desired culture is communicated, delivered through processes and procedures, and measured for progress.

And, to achieve this, the CEO must have emotional intelligence and social intelligence. Both a brutally honest assessment, and control, of their own thought processes, emotions and reactions; and a highly developed sensitivity to contexts and the interactions of others. But most of all the CEO has to have commitment to the people within the organisation.

The tenure of a CEO in the role is often short. Inevitably short-term results seem more important to them to the detriment of ensuring that they have built a culture that can sustain success. This is the fertile ground for creating Casual Leaders going forward. Low priority and low attention to developing a cadre of leaders that demonstrate the right behaviours, deliver the right culture and develop the people within the organisation. It is time that the CEOs were held accountable, and were measured and rewarded for creating the right culture in their organisation.

CREATING AN ENGAGED CULTURE

THE RESPONSIBILITY OF THE BOARD FOR CULTURE

"CULTURE EATS STRATEGY FOR BREAKFAST"

Goleman's and Albrecht's research backs up this famous quote attributed to the inimitable Peter Drucker. It does not matter how finely tuned and competitively advantaged the strategy is if the culture is not healthy and aligned. So you would think that this would preoccupy the chair, the CEO and the board. After all, the FRC clearly makes the CEO accountable and also holds the board responsible too.

21. The focus on culture needs to be continuous. Periodic reflection on whether the culture continues to be relevant in a changing environment can help the company adapt its culture to ensure it continues to support the company's success. The board is expected to assess and monitor culture for alignment with purpose and values."
61. The chair's role includes setting a board agenda primarily focussed on strategy, performance, value creation, culture... etc.
– FRC Guidance on Board Effectiveness, 2018

NB Of course, only main boards include a separate chairperson role. These duties within an operating board fall to the CEO.

And yet, research conducted by *Board Agenda* magazine, in conjunction with Mazars and INSEAD, produced some startling evidence to the contrary in a report entitled "Board Leadership in Corporate Culture: European Report 2017". This was a research study of 450 board members across Europe, including both listed and privately owned companies. Among the findings are these startling results:

o   Culture is the third highest priority after strategy and financial performance.
o   And setting the right tone from the top of the organisation is the main way to influence culture.

And yet:

o   56% of respondents said too little time was given to talk on cultural issues, with a further 15% saying that it was not valued enough as a topic to spend much time on.
o   32% said they did not have much information on actual culture to measure alignment with desired culture.
o   29% of respondents said they were not clear on the desired culture as there had been limited or no discussion.
o   17% said it was not measured at all.
o   16% of respondents said the culture is never discussed by the board.
o   And only 11% claimed they were clear on purpose, culture and long-term strategy and that these were actively checked to make sure they were aligned.

For me, what was even more alarming was the sources by which these directors measure culture in practice. The number one source was employee surveys. And then they relied on customer complaints and "risk events" (such as HR issues and rule breaches or compliance monitoring) or the results of employment tribunals or whistle-blowing. While McClelland and Goleman claim to show demonstrably better financial results from Authoritative leadership and positive culture, our boards do not measure for the opportunity – they just measure to evaluate the risk.

So in summary: although culture is important and the board agrees that they should set the right tone, many don't know what it is or what it should be, and the majority don't discuss it enough or measure it effectively.

What gets measured gets improved. If you are not creating the metrics, how seriously do you consider the subject? There are metrics galore on everything else including competitor benchmarks and tracking of progress over time.

○ **Andy Rule #1**
   If something is wrong in a business culture, you never have to look far from the top – the CEO.

○ **Andy Rule #2**
   Most companies are far too casual about their employees. Their managers and directors do not value them and spend little time trying to maximise their potential – they only pay lip service to any claim that people are their most important asset.

But what is "culture" anyway? The Oxford Dictionary defines culture as *"The ideas, customs and behaviour of a particular people or society"* and defines society as *"An organisation or club formed for a particular purpose or activity".*

Culture in this context is the behaviour of an organisation for a particular purpose. So why is it that our CEOs and our boards are not saying to themselves, "What sort of culture do we have?" and, "What sort of society should we be creating for this organisation?"

I cannot believe that any board thinks that they need a culture that is hostile or inefficient, or uncooperative and not working as a team, or where Casual Leaders in the hierarchy destroy morale, motivation and commitment. Surely the CEO and board want a culture that is fair, where advancement is merited, where rewards match accomplishment; where people are happy to stay and outsiders are keen to join, where the potential of their employees is developed and productivity increases as a result.

The chair, CEO and board have to think, "What sort of society do we want to create?" Currently, they are all missing the point – and the opportunity.

If you don't know what you have as a culture and don't know what behaviours you need as an organisation to build sustainability, all you will end up with is inefficiency and unhealthy behaviours. Nature abhors a vacuum but people want to know what "good" looks like. If the CEO and board don't tell them, people will invent their own rules. And this is how the Casual Leaders exist in organisations. They are inventing the rules of the house, either deliberately or unconsciously, and in so doing betraying the Social Contract and abusing the Work Contract. And yet many boards either leave their organisational culture unmanaged or see it as part of the function of the HR department and take neither accountability nor responsibility for it.

Whatever culture an organisation has, or should have, those behaviours do not supersede those of the Social Contract. The organisation is part of wider society and not more important than it. Therefore the behaviours of an organisation should only reinforce the rules of society and highlight those that benefit the organisation reaching its potential.

So what types of culture exist in organisations? Academic papers published in the *Harvard Business Review* at the start of 2018, under the title "The Culture Factor", suggest that there are eight types of corporate culture. Researchers and analysts Groysberg, Lee, Price and Cheng reviewed the findings from over a hundred commonly used social and behavioural models to build their own framework. Their model used two axes: "How People Interact" and "How People Respond to Change" and plotted eight distinct styles, which organisations were asked to identify with.

Two cultural styles were dominant:

o **"Results"** – where goal achievement is emphasised and people are motivated by a meritocracy built on capability and success. Eighty-nine per cent of companies surveyed self-identified this as part of their culture.

o **"Caring"** – which focusses on relationships and trust. Here people help and support each other as the emphasis is on sincerity and teamwork. Sixty-three per cent of organisations self-identified this as part of their culture.

The third most recognisable culture was "Order" but only 15% of respondents identified with it. Here the culture is focussed on respect, structure and shared norms. Employees want to fit in and are united by co-operation while leaders emphasise process and customs. Interestingly no other style scored more than 9% but these culture styles, along with "Order", were superior in "employee engagement" and "customer orientation". "Results" and "Caring" cultures, on the other hand, performed best for "differentiation" and "cost leadership". So if "Results" and "Caring" truly are the dominant corporate styles, then relying on employee engagement surveys and customer feedback are probably inadequate in measuring the culture anyway.

The reality is that it does not matter what theoretical culture style an organisation and its leaders identify as being theirs; sometimes this is pure aspiration and they are in denial as they mark their own homework. In practice I have found that there is more than one culture in any case. While there may well be a prevailing organisational culture which sets the environment or context, there are often many different cultures present. This is particularly true of an organisation that is spread over several sites, such as retailing or manufacturing, or where one team works predominantly outside of the office, such as field sales. Here, leaders can try to work within the confines of an organisation to try and create their own "Circle of Safety" as Simon Sinek describes.

○ **Andy Rule #3**
You can have the worst job in the world, but a good boss will make it a great job.

It is true however that the prevailing culture of the organisation has an enormous effect on whatever an individual leader might set out to do. Personally, I have orientation to both "Results" and "Caring" styles, and see the merits of each, particularly if merged to capture two important dynamics.

In the 1980s, the management consultant Claude Lineberry developed a model for the Energy/Attitude dynamic in organisational cultures. This has been adopted widely by people such as Dr Donald Tosti, in his pioneering work in behavioural psychology and organisational change, and Percy Barnevik, the highly successful CEO of Asea Brown Boveri in the 1990s.

I have found this model useful in understanding cultures, individuals and resistance to change.

LINEBERRY'S ENERGY INVESTMENT MODEL

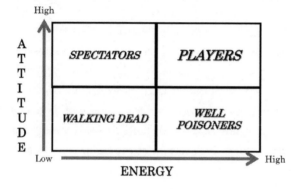

The Walking Dead are people with negative attitudes but very little energy to act. They moan, they tut, they sigh, they shake their heads, they shrug their shoulders, but are broadly compliant. They appear minimally engaged with the organisation; they are just doing their jobs and little more. They became like this because they have been repeatedly rejected or ridiculed in the past, often in public. They feel of no value or interest to their bosses or even their colleagues. This group are sometimes called Deadbeats or Deadwood, but the Walking Dead is damning enough in my opinion.

Spectators are "yes-men". They talk a lot but put little effort into actively doing anything. While they talk positively of their jobs and the organisation, they are not fully engaged. They are all in favour of action as long as it is down to someone else. They will seldom show initiative. In fact they will seldom take action, particularly if it involves doing something new or different – unless they are sure it is "safe" and beyond criticism or failure. But they will watch interestedly from the side-lines. At heart these people have good souls but need to be encouraged to bring out their energy. Sometimes this group is called Politicians!

Well Poisoners are people with highly negative attitudes but lots of energy. They are usually competent but disillusioned and have become active resisters to change. Their conversations tend to be about why what's proposed will not work. They are highly critical, go into minutiae and find fault. Frequently they blame others and find fault with their jobs, policies and the organisation but not with themselves. They are happy to review failed initiatives at length, recapping why they failed and how they knew they were going to fail if only someone had asked them. As they are capable, with high energy, they can become particularly difficult to deal with unless their attitude is changed. They could make a significant contribution but, because of their behaviour and attitude, they get sidelined and create resentment around them. This group is sometimes called Cynics!

Players are the high-performing group. They have positive attitudes and the energy to match. They see the benefits that the organisation is trying to achieve and are willing investors of effort to help make it happen. They invest considerable effort in both doing the job well and in making things better. These are the people who think they can make a difference and often do. This group go beyond the job description and are the most likely to seek increased responsibility. They are the people who anticipate problems and show the initiative in offering solutions or in improving processes. They collaborate with their colleagues and make sure information is shared. Effective teamwork is second nature to them. They want to be the best they can be and actively seek out training opportunities for themselves. They are open to both new ideas and feedback on their own performance. The words they use are positive and inclusive such as "yes", "we" and "us".

The typical make-up of these people within an organisation may surprise you. In their paper "Making Players Out of Spectators, Cynics and Deadwood", Dr Donald Tosti and Fred Nikols reveal that there has been an attempt to estimate precisely this. They reference Vanguard Consulting, who reviewed the data they had collated from over 2,000 managers and estimated the proportion of each typology within organisations as:

Players – 14%
Well Poisoners – 39%
Spectators – 38%
Walking Dead – 9%

No wonder so few organisations are in an engaged health state!

The worst colleague I have ever had was a Well Poisoner. Nathan was a purchasing director and the longest-serving member of the board. He actively resisted the majority of proposals for the organisation over the course of several years. In fact he behaved like a saboteur in many ways by trying to stall progress, repeal the decision or actively undermine initiatives. If he did not agree with a board decision he would constantly reopen the debate at every opportunity, even as actions were being progressed, and would never take collective responsibility. He would deny debates had happened if he continued to disagree with decisions. He obsessed over his own hobby horse theories, once asking the same question in seven meetings in a row despite full and respectful responses and being given all the background data that supported a proposal. He displayed positivity only when it was his own idea, but was fully compliant with any proposal imposed by the group headquarters as he was paranoid at losing his own job.

Unfortunately this colleague's behaviours went unchecked. Nathan had appointed himself as the main critic of everyone else and used emotive language, claiming data and research had been falsified if he didn't agree or if it challenged his own output. It was almost impossible to reason with him as he switched from "critical parent" to "child" ego-states and rarely could sustain "adult" mode. He had some of the traits of the narcissist in that: he demanded recognition of all his achievements, never reciprocating in return; he was highly sensitive to criticism; and he alternated between bullying and charm to pursue his own goals. He had no problem distorting the truth – "That never happened" – and when confronted with evidence would claim it had been invented. He combined it with a Coercive leadership style with his team and other departments. He had no sense of contributing as a team player and working together collaboratively; consulting and informing other departments were foreign concepts for him as he took arbitrary actions on a whim. This in turn had knock-on effects to the entire corporate culture. His behaviour was corrosive and of such attrition that individuals and whole departments become defensive and uncooperative with their own activity. They became the Walking Dead or Spectators. Nathan was a Casual Leader of the worst type and in a position of power within the organisation.

Sadly he is not the only example. I know of a purchasing director in a different company who exhibited similar if less extreme behaviours. Richie used to boast of his achievements as loudly as possible – "The deal of the century". Unfortunately these were often exposed as exaggerations as competitor benchmarks showed that they had better deals. However, he was highly critical of others. When the marketing director tried to list a traditional product for the most conservative markets, Richie went round the business openly describing the product as "mediaeval" and the marketing director as "a dinosaur". Market data and trials validated the product, and, despite Richie's attempts to recruit collaborators to sabotage the proposal, the product was launched to immediate success. Eventually Richie was sacked for trying to recruit resistance to an office relocation.

Both Nathan and Richie contributed to the unhealthy states of their respective corporate cultures. They damaged morale and the success of the business. Both validated their actions in the belief they were just providing challenge, but they did it in the wrong way and failed to support any but their own teams. Neither felt any guilt or remorse for their behaviour and impact on others. It may be that their own frustration at lack of career progression contributed to their mindsets and behaviour. But I think that they had crippling low self-esteem also, like so many bullies, and needed to shore up their sense of self-worth by eroding other people's.

Just as the CEO is a role model and should set a positive example in behaviours to the rest of the organisation, so should each and every member of the board. They must emulate the leadership style and decision-making process of the CEO; they must be united behind the strategy and show a cohesive presentation of the board; they should actively demonstrate the best example of team-working to the organisation; they must embody not just the literal values of the organisation but be seen to abide by the spirit of those values too. Each member of the board must be a "player" – bringing positive energy and attitude to every interaction within and outside the organisation. And finally, they must take responsibility for the culture of the organisation and the people that make it live and breathe. They are the eyes and ears of the CEO throughout the hierarchy and should have zero tolerance for Casual Leaders under their authority and their negative impact on morale. It is a neglect of responsibility to claim that they have no time or data to measure culture or create the right working environment for their employees.

CULTURE HEALTH STATES

In reality, whatever the prevailing culture might be, there are four distinct **health states** for an organisation and I have experienced all of them:

1   **Engaged health state:** People are united by a common purpose and understand their role in achieving it. The goals are stretching but achievable and they have control on how to progress them. Support and training are evident. Equipment is fit for purpose. Employees feel respected and valued; their accomplishments are recognised and rewarded. There is an atmosphere of mutual trust and respect. The Social and Work Contracts are symbiotic. Innovative thought and creativity are encouraged. The workforce is balanced between introverts and extroverts. Staff turnover is moderate: there is a healthy balance of new blood while experience is maintained. Teamwork is seamless; co-operation and information-sharing are high. Processes and procedures are efficient and respected. Individuals are committed and both emotional and social intelligence are highly developed. Most of the managers and leaders are "Players"; the energy of people is high and the attitude is "can do" positivity.

2 **Ambivalent health state:** Purpose and role are readily understood but the targets are unrealistic in their ambition. While support and training are available there is a gap between corporate ambition and the reasons to believe that the planned actions of the organisation will shift in performance to meet it. The Social and Work Contracts are abided by but leaders punish mistakes. Innovation, creativity and energy are stifled – "That's not how things are done around here". While you can be punished for making a decision, there are no consequences for not making one! Processes are inefficient and bureaucratic as papers are shuffled and committees convened – anything to avoid taking responsibility for action. Deadlines constantly move backwards as only the perfect solution, with minimal risk, will be approved. Office politics and prevarication thrives. People are compliant but not engaged. The workforce are characterised as "lifers", as after the initial years of new blood, turnover of staff stagnates. Many people are "Spectators". Energy is low and attitude is "We could try that sometime later."

3 **Chaotic health state:** Purpose and roles are unclear; responsibility and accountability is debatable. Priorities are constantly superseded; workloads and deadlines are intense but processes and procedures are discouraged and distrusted. Teamwork and co-operation are impaired; people trip over each other, believing that they are both in charge of an action. Trust is low. Action is the order of the day as long as you do what the leader wants. You are told what the creativity and innovation should be. Targets are stretching but support and training are non-existent. People are seen as expendable. Energy is high but alignment is wayward leading to inefficiency. Morale is low and the Social and Work Contracts are abused. Staff turnover is high

due to the attritional nature of day-to-day business. Attitude is "Just do something, anything, but do it now."

4 **Toxic health state:** It all starts with one person – a Casual Leader. S/he displays many of the "toxic" behaviours detailed by Karl Albrecht. These have a toxic effect which poisons the behaviour of others. If s/he is high in rank s/he will recruit similar Casual Leaders and the poisonous behaviours infect the whole organisation like an epidemic. Even when the originator has gone their cancerous effects remain and this is the hardest culture to shift back to a healthy state. A toxic culture is displayed across a wide spectrum. Initially it may just be negative relationships and dysfunctional teams. However, if unchecked it will spiral. The atmosphere will become quieter and more furtive. Purpose and roles will become vague. At its worst it will manifest itself as institutional. Targets are unachievable and many don't know what they are as internal communication is poor. Deadlines are intense and workloads are high, with little control or discretion in how to execute them. Support is missing and behaviours are ungoverned. Rewards are low and consequences are absent. There is no respect or trust within the organisation. Processes and procedures are missing. Work is characterised by turf wars, hobby horses, pettiness and defensiveness. Individual directors and departments are dysfunctional and make arbitrary decisions with no consultation of or communication to colleagues. Teamwork is non-existent as departments retreat into silos; co-operation and information-sharing are negligible and grudging. People rely on immediate colleagues to survive. Training and support are not encouraged or evident. Skills and equipment are insufficient. Development and advancement are negligible; personal ambition is not encouraged. Promises are not kept. The Social Contract is

abused and the Work Contract is seen by employees as an onerous commitment. Over time, introverts are the dominant profile of employees; emotional and social intelligence are highly limited. Casual Leaders are everywhere, usually Well Poisoners who use Coercive or Pacesetting styles, abusing the Social Contract. The workforce shrivels in energy to be dominated by the Walking Dead or Spectators. Staff turnover is low and the workforce dominated by "lifers". Selfishness rules. Leaders' assertiveness becomes aggression as frustrated by the apathy of employees whose attitude is "can't do" or "won't do". By this stage the survivors within the organisation think this is the normal state of affairs that would be in any other place. They have been desensitised and resigned themselves to deeply unhealthy relationships and institutionalised behaviours.

Even if you aspire to have an Authoritative leadership style yourself, trying to achieve that in any organisation which is not in the "engaged" health state is exhausting as you are pushing water uphill!

Unless the organisation is a new start-up, each CEO and board will have inherited one of these health states as their organisation's culture. And some boards might be part of a wider structure such as a conglomerate, a global organisation or a public body of the government. They might well be subject to a Coercive or Pacesetting leadership style themselves from higher up the hierarchy. Or they may have inherited a mixed bag of cultures due to mergers and acquisitions as many organisations are in environments which have to consolidate suppliers to survive external threats. In which case there could be internal forces and inequities which also bring pressure to bear on the culture that they are responsible for. That's life and that's reality. But to not recognise and do something about that is irresponsible and they are failing in their duty. If their view is that there are more important things to do, or that they cannot afford the time or cost, my view is that they cannot afford not to.

Of course, accurately understanding the culture of a business is difficult. Frequently the CEO's interactions are with a reduced number of people who all have their own agenda and the CEO is in danger of falling for the "Queen effect". This states that the Queen must believe the world smells of paint, as everywhere she goes it has just been freshly decorated to give her the best impression! So CEOs can be in ignorance or even denial over the actual health state of the culture unless they have put in place effective processes and measurements of culture. More on this later.

I do know of one CEO who deliberately created a chaotic health state in their company. Stephen was probably motivated by his own Coercive leadership style and ensuring there were no power brokerages within the organisation to challenge his authority. It was a style that he had experienced earlier in his own career and he adopted it for himself; such is the insidious influence of negative role models. It certainly gave him decisive powers and short-term results as he overcame inherited apathy and ineptitude. However, I believe in the long term those results have not been sustainable as the talent, potential and commitment of his employees have been frittered away. Certainly morale of the organisation was low, with high incidences of stress-related illnesses such as anxiety and depression.

I would expect most CEOs and boards to accept that efficiency and productivity are key to their responsibilities. And, after ensuring the competency of individuals, the key is to create a culture that drives teamwork. Certainly none of the eight corporate cultures identified in "The Culture Factor" suggests that teamwork is dispensable, even if "Results" has a greater focus on the individual rather than interdependency. A healthy and engaged culture must rely on efficient collaboration, co-operation and information-sharing, and there are a number of ways to ensure this, which will also give effective measurement of actual behaviours and progress to the desired culture.

Part of the answer is clearly to determine the optimum behaviours or values of an organisation to achieve its purpose as fast as possible. And I will explore these behaviours and how to select the most appropriate for an organisation later in the book. But there is one particular behaviour which must be counterproductive in the vast majority of organisations and hierarchical structures. And this is a behaviour that organisations have been particularly insensitive to with the rise of an educated, younger, female and more diverse workforce entering traditional organisations dominated by older white men. This behaviour is best understood as the difference between assertiveness and aggression, and organisations need to get a grip of the difference sooner rather than later.

For the vast majority of organisations and cultures, aggression is a destructive behaviour. It does not matter how competitive a situation or environment is, or desired to be; aggression will not bring out the best in people within an organisation. As we will discuss later, aggression might be a desirable or admirable attribute in some rare circumstances, but even then it is best be directed outside the organisation. Many people fail to make this distinction.

The Oxford English Dictionary defines aggression as follows:

o **1.** Feelings of anger or antipathy resulting in hostile or violent behaviour; readiness to attack or confront.
o **1.1** The action of attacking without provocation.
o **1.2** Forcefulness.

Assertiveness is quite a different thing and can be a positive and desired competence in many organisations. This is the quality of being confident and self-assured without being aggressive.

It allows people to state their point of view without either threatening others or being submissive and without being ignored or denying their opinion a voice.

The tipping point between aggression and assertiveness can be the emotion behind the forcefulness of a response. This displays the level of control a person has over their own emotions and the level of respect they have for others. In practice, I have found that a number of men in particular cannot make this distinction as events unfold and this has a significant negative effect. Often, while the words might be contained appropriately, the tone of voice and the body language shows a need to dominate and subjugate others with threatening postures, e.g. harsh and clipped intonation, raised voices, red faces, glaring, standing over people, balling their fists, leaning into others to make them feel uncomfortable etc.

The impact of aggression on others is expressed well in the Drama Triangle. Stephen Karpman was a student of transactional analysis under Eric Berne. In 1968, he wrote an article on the social model of destructive interaction and illustrated it as below.

The model shows personal responsibility and power within interactions. Karpman defined three roles:

KARPMAN DRAMA TRIANGLE
(WHEN ATTITUDE IS WRONG)

- Aggressive
- "It's all your fault"

Persecutor ←→ **Rescuer**

- Look after
- "Let me help you"

No two people sit in the same position at any one time

Victim

- Defensive
- "Poor me"

1 The Persecutor (or the Bully)
   Blames everyone else for problems. Controlling, dominating, criticising, oppressive, angry, resentful and superior. Puts others down. Has all the rights while others have none.
2 The Victim (or Helpless)
   A defensive position. Feels victimised, helpless, hopeless, trapped, ashamed, guilty, powerless, dependent. Seeks others to make decisions and to solve problems.
3 The Rescuer (or the Martyr)
   A classic enabler, the Rescuer gains self-esteem by helping others. Tries to be considerate and selfless but feels the need to fix problems. Yet the act of rescuing can be negative as it keeps the Victim helpless and dependent. It is also an excuse for the Rescuer not to address their own issues and anxiety.

Karpman's observation was that the triangle starts when a person takes on either the role of Victim or Persecutor. This then compels them to enlist others into a different position. The triangle is then perpetuated, with people occupying different positions until the interaction is completed. Sometimes the Victim can turn on the Rescuer, who then switches to being the Persecutor. In all it becomes a toxic set of behaviours, with attack, defence and counter-attack as the dynamic of the interaction.

Some researchers have argued that the Persecutors are more likely to be in leadership positions leading to culture characteristics of blame, fear, and manipulation with the result of high staff turnover. A Victim-led culture would have low morale and low engagement and show avoidance of conflict, while a Rescuer culture would also be negative with a high dependency on the leader, low innovation and low initiative.

In 1990, the Australian psychologist Acey Choy proposed an alternative model as an antithesis to the Drama Triangle –

the Winner's Triangle. This shows that by adopting different attitudes and behaviours a positive interaction can be developed which does not have the drama games shown by Karpman.

THE WINNERS TRIANGLE

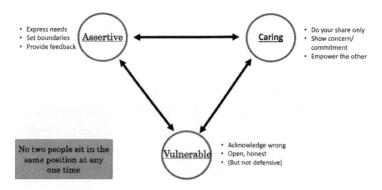

This model relies on high levels of both emotional intelligence and social intelligence. Through this self-awareness, personal responsibility is retained and boundaries are kept to ensure the Assertive do not become Persecutors and the Caring do not become Rescuers. The Vulnerable are encouraged to accept their position, think through options and alternatives, and go onto problem-solve for themselves. The Assertive can remain challenging and express their needs but avoid behaviours which are punishing of others, while the Caring allow others to enable themselves whilst still offering vital support, positioning themselves more in a coaching style through active listening rather than volunteering solutions.

The identification, awareness and maintenance of these barriers are essential to deliver a healthy culture. If the barriers are upheld then people can meet their needs while remaining respected and valued. Their skills and potential can be exercised and developed. But if the barriers are not recognised or ignored the culture immediately becomes unhealthy and will degenerate into a toxic environment.

A summary of the evidence so far can be seen overleaf.

But this still does not tell us HOW to create the right culture!

Characteristics	ENGAGED HEALTH STATE	CHAOTIC OR TOXIC HEALTH STATE
CEO Ego-state	Adult	Critical parent
CEO Motivation	Achievement	Power
CEO Vision	Broad context within society as a whole	Narrow context; organisation only
CEO Leadership Style	Authoritative style used most often	Coercive or Pacesetting styles used most often
CEO Tone of Voice	Approachable, inclusive and engaging	Distant, exclusive, tell and direct
CEO Behaviours	Conscious and value-led; Social & Work Contracts respected; high recognition and praise; listen first, talk last; authority delegated; optimal decision-making demonstrated	Value less; Social and Work contracts abused; highly critical; talk first, don't listen; authority hoarded; decision-making arbitrary
Board Members	Support CEO style and strategy; demonstrate positive team-working	Visibly different in style and tone; act independently of each other and CEO
Culture Type	Mix of "Results", "Caring" and "Order"; progress measured	"Results" only
Organisation Model	Support and challenge	Challenge only
Manager profile	Positive role models; "Assertive" and "Caring"	Casual Leaders; Aggressive; "Persecutors"
Employees Attitude	Adult ego-state; "Players" dominate; High trust; leadership followers	Adapted child ego-state; "Well Poisoners" and "Spectators"; low trust; listless workers.
Behaviours of Employees	"Caring" and "Vulnerable"; high teamwork	"Rescuers" and "Victims"; poor collaboration

IT'S NOT LIFE AND DEATH!

What's all the fuss? For most organisations it is not about life and death, although low commitment, poor collaboration and weak communication could well put people at risk of physical harm.

There are of course some organisations where it is exactly that though – a matter of life and death. These organisations' very purpose does put their employees at high risk of personal, physical and psychological harm. Here, effective leadership and efficient teamwork are essential to achieve their goals. It is not a matter left to chance and they have put significant work into forging the right culture over centuries to achieve these goals. And, while they may not always get it right, these organisations are widely respected and held in high esteem. So what can we learn from them?

I am of course referring to the armed forces, whom we trust to keep us safe and to preserve our way of life from external threats. Highly professional, highly proficient, these organisations have created comprehensive and effective models to recruit and train the right people to become their leaders and to create the right culture. This approach is imperative as these leaders have to mesh with an equally highly trained workforce of specialists and create effective teams.

On reviewing the processes of several of these organisations it is possible to detect common themes that show their approach, from which others can learn.

Firstly, all armed forces have a rigorous selection process to identify their future officers and then train them exhaustively. It is not enough to have the ambition to be an officer and the commitment to work hard.

The US Marine Corps has a particularly rigorous selection process *before* an application is accepted. To be even selected candidates will already have had to pass several tests including: an interview, a written essay, identity and background checks, supplying five references, passing a rigorous medical exam, and meeting the standards of a physical fitness test. If candidates are successful they are enrolled then for a ten- to twelve-week course at the Officer Candidate School (OCS). Despite the detailed screening process, attrition rates are as high as 30–50% at OCS as standards are so exacting. On successful completion of OCS, officers are appointed as 2nd Lieutenants but still do not go on to active service.

New officers need to complete their officer training at The Basic School (TBS). Training at TBS takes a further twenty-eight weeks on the Basic Officer Course, which has five horizontal themes that define the expectations of an officer: (1) exemplary character; (2) 24/7 devotion to leadership; (3) ability to decide, communicate and act; (4) competence with an offensive mindset; (5) mentally strong & physically tough. Even on graduating from TBS, successful officers go on to attend further schools in various specialties before being assigned to an active unit.

Of course the US Marine Corps wants leaders that have the right mental and physical capacity, and need to train candidates in weapons, tactics and technology. But the most important thing they are looking for are the right leadership traits – the character of the candidate. In her book *Backbone*, Julia Dyer summarises the US Marine Corps leadership traits with the acronym

JJDIDTIEBUCKLE. The training has been in leadership environments in stressful situations and the instructors are looking for these essential leadership characteristics:

o Justice – being fair and consistent
o Judgement – the 70% solution to deliver fast actions (70% knowledge, 70% analysis and 70% confidence)
o Dependability – do what you say when you say
o Initiative – improvise, adapt, and overcome
o Decisiveness
o Tact – communication that reflects the audience and enhances comprehension
o Integrity – honesty, a desire to inspire and a devotion to values
o Endurance
o Bearing – setting an example in attitude, behaviour and drive
o Unselfishness
o Courage – doing what's right under stress and pressure
o Knowledge – beyond the facts of the job to include context and self-awareness
o Loyalty – to your command; both to subordinates and to superior officers
o Enthusiasm – focussed on positive energy and willing to make sacrifices.

The British Armed Forces have similar processes and training schools. The British Army use an Army Officer Selection Board while the Royal Navy use the Admiralty Interview Board. Army officer candidates have to have a good education, be physically fit and be sponsored. Those considered suitable attend a two-day test of mental aptitude, group participation, planning exercises and a battery of interviews. Only after passing this, and a detailed vetting process, are they selected to attend the Army

Officer Selection Board, where they then have to pass a variety of academic, physical, mental and aptitude tests over four days. Just as with the US Marines, the boards are identifying candidates with leadership potential. They are looking for motivation, moral compass, values, standards and the desire to take responsibility. Successful candidates will have to display the essential character traits that each armed service has identified for their officer cadre. Every year up to 3,000 candidates apply but as few as 700 will go onto Sandhurst for training as a regular army officer.

The British Army has published these traits as the Army Leadership Code, which consists of seven leadership behaviours:

1   Lead by example
2   Encourage thinking
3   Apply reward and discipline
4   Demand high performance
5   Encourage confidence in the team
6   Recognise individual strengths and weaknesses
7   Strive for team goals

While the Royal Navy has a list of twelve leadership traits:

1   Capacity for judgement and decision-making
2   Cheerfulness
3   Clarity and vision
4   Communication skills
5   Confidence
6   Humanity and humility
7   Innovation
8   Integrity
9   Moral and physical courage
10 Professional knowledge
11 Stamina
12 Trust

Only after successfully passing these boards are candidates invited to the respective officer training schools – a forty-four-week course at Royal Military Academy Sandhurst for the Army; or a thirty-week course at the Britannia Royal Naval Training College. The training is designed to expand each cadet's character, intellect and professional skills with continuous emphasis on leadership training as well as acquiring practical skills for warfare.

The Sandhurst motto is "Serve to Lead" and it is the only academy where the instructors are largely senior non-commissioned officers or warrant officers. It teaches above all else that an officer must lead through unselfish example and that leadership of personnel is a privilege. Again, despite the screening process, the attrition rate is high – typically 20% of cadets drop out of Sandhurst over the training period. It has been calculated that, even with shorter commissioning courses for the Army Reserve and professionally qualified cadets (e.g. doctors, dentists, lawyers etc.), only 30% of those who aspire to be a British Army officer will be successfully commissioned.

For elite forces the tests of character are even more strenuous. One SAS veteran told me that potential officers have to undergo "Officer Week" in addition to the famously demanding physical process all candidates undergo. In this process, potential officers are given command tasks on various operational scenarios. This is to assess how tiredness and lack of sleep impacts on their thought processes. Candidates may not have an infantry background but they have to show they can achieve positive outcomes from the given tasks. Then they debrief both the commanding officer and the senior non-commissioned officers. Standards are exacting from both the superior officer and the troops the candidate hopes to lead. I am told the attrition rate of this process can be as high as 100% – "Better to have NO officers than to have unsuitable ones," the veteran said to me.

This is a highly effective method to capture 360-degree feedback and ensure a rounded assessment of performance. It must surely lead to raised levels of self-awareness and put the emotional and social intelligence of the candidate under intense scrutiny. But it does not stop there. The SAS veteran tells me that, even if found suitable, a new officer is expected to look and learn *for a year* before thinking they could have an input into operations!

At the heart of these examples of leadership traits are two common themes: the leaders need to be role models in their behaviour, and they must possess both emotional and social intelligence to be effective leaders.

The second thing all armed forces have in common is a thorough induction process within the training period. This is beyond the professional and practical skills they need as modern practitioners of warfare. This is about understanding the history and heritage of the organisations they have joined.

All officer candidates, in each armed service, are educated in the detailed histories of their chosen organisations and how they have forged and protected their country. They are immersed in the facts, the folklore and legends of individual heroes, the battle honours and particularly glorious engagements. They are educated in the idiosyncrasies and customs that are embedded in each culture. They are taught to identify with the past, taking pride in how that has created the organisation as it is today and they are encouraged to commit to similar behaviours to reinforce their identity into future engagements. It is immersion in the role models of the past so that they may become role models in the present.

For the US Marines there are a number of affectionate nicknames that are used by the American public: "Jarhead", "Leatherneck" or "Devil Dogs". But the Corps themselves recruit under the slogan "The Few, The Proud" and prefer to be known as the "First to Fight", having been in more than 300 beach landings in their 250-year history.

One of the most famous US Marine customs is the observance of the Marine Corps Birthday as they recognise the resolution to form them on 10th November 1775. Celebrations include a reading from the Marine Corps Manual and a birthday message from the commandant; the cutting of a birthday cake by the commanding officer; and the presentation of the first and second pieces of cake to the oldest and youngest present.

Winston Churchill was said to have dismissed the customs of the Royal Navy as "nothing but rum, sodomy and the lash", but it is highly unlikely he did so. The Royal Navy are proud of their history as the "Senior Service" within the UK armed forces and was once the most powerful force in the world. There are so many traditions associated with the Navy, stretching back through a glorious history, that it is impossible to give more than a flavour of them. There are separate rules for which flags fly, and where on the ship, dependent on time of day and whether the ship is at sea; there are separate badges to identify individual ships, submarines, squadrons and shore establishments; and there are two unique games that are played by the Navy when off duty – a board game called Uckers and a card game called Euchers. Perhaps the most famous custom is giving the "Loyal Toast" to the monarch in the officers' mess whilst seated, due to the historically low head height on board. This is followed by the youngest officer proposing a different toast dependent on what day of week it is, e.g. Sunday is "absent friends", Wednesday is "ourselves".

Sandhurst itself has its own ceremonies, formal dinners and the famous Sovereign's Parade to mark the passing-out of newly commissioned officers. One tradition is that each training company is named after a famous battle or campaign in which the British Army has fought. There might be as many as ten such companies training at any point in time and the names change each year. Officer cadets will have been selected by a regiment in their second term at Sandhurst as the British Army is still founded on the regimental system. And each regiment has a unique history and identity expressed in a myriad of detail: the regimental colours or flags; the uniforms, insignia and badges (such as the famous red berets, parachute wings and Pegasus patch of the Parachute Regiment); mascots (such as the Irish wolfhound for the Irish Guards; or the goat that represents the Royal Welsh Fusiliers, a good-luck symbol said to date back to either the American War of Independence or the Crimean War); anniversaries or celebrations which may be as quirky as the presentation of leeks to warrant officers of the Welsh Guards on St David's Day, or the presentation of shamrocks by the Royal Family to the Irish Guards on St Patrick's Day to mark their conduct in the Boer War. Many regiments even have their own regimental march music.

For British Army veterans, active service on Christmas Day holds many fond memories. Traditionally, troops are woken up to a cup of "gunfire", which is black tea generously laced with rum, served to them in bed by their officers. This drink has been traced back to the 1890s and its origin was to give soldiers Dutch courage before morning attacks. Later in the day, an effort is put on to give a Christmas feast, which again was often served to the troops by their own officers as they sit down together.

All of these customs, no matter which armed service you join, have a serious purpose. They serve to create an identity. Something unique and unifying, a common bond for the participants, and the start to building an essential esprit de corps. These customs create a sense of a proud tradition in which individuals are now included, and to which they have to live up to in the present and the future.

Another observation is that all armed services have identified their values, a common code of behaviour that is expected of all marines, soldiers, sailors or aircrew regardless of rank. This is the base standard expected of everyone, even though officers have to exhibit the leadership traits as well.

The US Marines proudly talk of just three values – honour, courage and commitment. While you would instinctively expect the last two, I was immediately struck by the first value as it is a word and concept that has largely disappeared in modern-day language and society. They define honour as follows: "This is the bedrock of our character. It is the quality that empowers Marines to exemplify the ultimate in ethical and moral behaviour: to never lie, cheat, or steal; to abide by an uncompromising code of integrity; to respect human dignity; and to have respect and concern for each other. It represents the maturity, dedication, trust and dependability that commits Marines to act responsibly, be accountable for their actions, fulfil their obligations, and hold others accountable for their actions."

But even their definition of "commitment" is surprising too. "It promotes the highest order of discipline for unit and self and is the ingredient that instils dedication to Corps and country 24 hours a day, pride, concern for others, and an unrelenting determination to achieve a standard of excellence in every endeavour. Commitment is the value that establishes the Marine as the warrior and citizen others strive to emulate."

WOW! Here is an organisation that sees the wider social context in which it works and sets out values that deliberately enshrines the Social Contract into their ethos! The US Marines are uncompromising in their ambition and the expectations of each marine to be a shining example of good citizenship by taking personal accountability for their behaviours. There is no room for a Casual Leader within these values!

The British Army extolls six values: courage, discipline, respect for others, integrity, loyalty and selfless commitment. Again, I was struck by their definitions. "Respect for others, both those inside and outside of our organisation, is not only a legal obligation, it is a fundamental principle of the freedom our society enjoys. Teams that embrace diversity, and value each individual for their contribution and viewpoint, are always stronger for it. We must treat everyone we encounter, as we would wish to be treated."

The British Army defines also a list of three standards by which to put their values into practice: appropriate behaviour (including mutual respect and avoidance of conduct that offends others) lawfulness, and total professionalism.

Here, again, is an organisation that recognises the wider social context within which it works. It recognises the Social Contract within its code of behaviour and puts great emphasis on the accountability of the individual and the forging of good teamwork.

The Royal Navy also recognises their place within society, although they put less emphasis on it, other than stating that the nation relies on them. However they publish six values which clearly show their commitment to each other's Social Contracts and to creating effective teams. They explain "respect" as follows: "Treating everyone fairly, with respect and dignity. Recognising that we are all different and using those differences to benefit the team. Eradicating bullying and harassment and valuing the contribution that every person makes to the team. Ensuring that all our people feel respected, valued and supported and that they play an essential role in the organisation."

The commonality in the codes of behaviour of all three armed services is striking. There is a recognition of the wider social context and the Social Contract. There is emphasis on personal accountability and the need to role-model specific behaviours which create mutual trust and respect. There is acknowledgement of the rights of the individual; the right to dignity and respect. And there is a recognition of the positive benefits of a duty of care to each other in forging effective teamwork despite differences of opinion, experience and ability.

A further observation is that all armed services clearly signal their approval of behaviour through the medal system.

In Britain there are numerous such medals that can be awarded across all armed forces personnel and even nursing staff or civilians that have contributed to a theatre of war. These cannot be applied for! You cannot nominate yourself or ask to be recognised. You have to be recommended for these awards and many of them are for conspicuous displays of courage or self-sacrifice or indeed leadership in the face of the enemy. There is obviously a pecking order for medals to signal the level of commitment and sacrifice being recognised and they are independent of rank or pay scale. Even if a medal is not considered warranted there is a range of other ways of recognising individuals through emblems such as "Mentioned in Despatches" or "Queen's Commendations". These awards are also published and held on the individual's service record. In addition, campaign medals can be awarded to show what theatre of operations an individual was involved in. Or if they have been involved for years in a number of operational campaigns, there is the "Accumulated Campaign Service" medal. The combination of these separate medals allows an individual to proudly display the recognition of their personal courage, leadership or operational deployment and in which parts of the world. It is a unique CV for each service person that is displayed as part of their uniform, effectively personalising it for all the world to see.

American armed forces have a similar system but go one step further with the inclusion of the Purple Heart. This is uniquely awarded to those personnel killed or wounded in the face of the enemy. Literally a badge showing that you have sacrificed your life or suffered harm to your body for your nation.

These awards are so effective in creating affiliation between the personnel regardless of rank that they have created their own unofficial versions called challenge coins. These mementoes are created by various groups to show that disparate teams have been pulled together and have successfully overcome operational challenges and hardships – a band of comrades with a shared experience. The benefit of these unofficial "campaign medals" is that they are earned and deserved regardless of which forces have combined to get a positive outcome – even from different countries and different armed services.

These systems of awards are conspicuous signs of approval and reward for behaviour in keeping with the values of the organisations they serve. They are not expensive. They do not accelerate promotion or rank. They carry public significance far beyond the traditional rewards that are awarded by most organisations which rely on title, salary or bonus recognition. And they link back to past holders of these awards showing a link and continuity with the role models of the past – creating a distinct fellowship of unique merit.

Finally, all armed forces have a rigid and legal code to enforce military discipline outside of the civil courts. Within the UK, the three armed forces are now served by one unitary legal body, the Military Court Service (MCS). The MCS's role is to carry out timely, impartial and efficient legal proceedings for the armed forces. Service personnel are subject to civil law but also to "service law". Service law includes all civil and criminal legislation but includes additional offences due to the emphasis on personal discipline and military duties. It recognises also that personnel may serve abroad and need the certainty of the same legal parameters wherever they offend. Interestingly, members of the armed forces do not have contracts of employment and much of the law which governs civilian employment does not apply to service personnel. Service law does, however, deal with a number of areas which are broadly similar to those that would be covered in a contract of employment, e.g. enlistment, discharge, terms and conditions of service, and the making of complaints.

As with any large body of society, there is a wide range of offences committed by armed services personnel right through the ranks. Offences can stretch from theft, fraud and assault through to mistreating a subordinate. And the sentences can include: admonishment, fines, prison terms and reduction in rank, through to dishonourable discharge from the service. While sentencing can result in a reduction in rank for non-commissioned officers I think it unlikely that more senior officers would suffer that fate. They are much more likely to be asked to resign their commission if guilty as they would no longer be judged credible in leading subordinates.

The fact is though that, regardless of rank, all armed forces personnel are held to a higher standard of behaviour and discipline than general society. There is a conscious effort to make justice impartial and to make it rigorous in application. There is a clear balance of reward versus consequence to ensure that appropriate behaviours are being demonstrated throughout the hierarchy.

So what lessons can other organisations learn from the armed services? I believe that there are a number of key lessons in how to create a cohesive, effective and healthy culture that is geared up to perform at the highest level.

○ **Rigorous recruitment on character not just competencies**
"There are a number of people with very good degrees out there – but what you are looking for is character." – General Nanson, Commandant of the Royal Military Academy Sandhurst.

All armed services are clear on the requirement of moral character to be selected into their leadership training. Their view is that there are some things that can be taught but if you do not have the right moral compass or you are ruled by selfishness, you will never be a Good Leader.

The uninitiated would expect a certain level of intelligence and physical fitness to be high on the requirements, but I find it noteworthy that the armed services place such high expectations on character, alongside the other criteria, that the rejection rates for applicants exceed 70%.

In contrast, most organisations I know put the emphasis on technical competencies and experience. These are probed in depth but discussion of leadership style, or size of previous teams, or experience of a variety of personnel challenges, are rarely explored. Many organisations do not bother with psychometric evaluation and rely purely on the subjective assessment of the interviewers. Even if evaluation techniques are used, I am unaware of any organisation which has a declared benchmark for character or team-working metrics across their organisation so again it is just a "gut feel" evaluation. When I asked one senior manager what their recruitment criteria had been historically the reply was, "Would they fit in with everyone else? Can I see myself enjoying a coffee with them?"

○ Set the highest values for your leaders

"The most important thing I learned is that soldiers watch what their leaders do. You can give them classes and lecture them forever, but it is your personal example they will follow." – General Colin Powell, ex-commander of US Army Forces Command and ex-chairman of the Joint Chiefs of Staff.

The armed services know that their leaders have to be role models and live by the highest possible standards. They want a high-performance cadre of leaders who behave as Lineberry's "Players". They cannot take the risk of Casual Leaders who behave as Well Poisoners or Spectators. And so they set much more exacting values for their leaders than the rank-and-file personnel. The emphasis is on personal accountability, and adult behaviours, with high emotional and social intelligence and a willingness to make personal sacrifices for those in your care. There are countless examples of leaders who inspired their troops for their personal character and their willingness to suffer the same hardships as the people under their command. Some of them are even well known to the general public outside of the armed services, e.g. Lieutenant Colonel Colin "Mad Mitch" Campbell Mitchell at Aden or General James "Mad Dog" Mattis and Colonel Tim Collins in Iraq. Through their own personal example they inspired their troops and generated enormous admiration and loyalty.

Many organisations I know do not make this distinction. If there are any values of the organisation, they are stated for everyone and there is no higher standard set for those in leadership positions.

In reality, many Casual Leaders take their status to excuse themselves from the standards and experiences expected of others. Instead of seeing their rank as a requirement to behave better and be an example, they see it as a privilege to do less, knowing they are less likely to be challenged. They don't suffer the same hardships or work as their teams but see it as beneath them to be involved at this level. The quality they demonstrate is selfishness not selflessness. Frequently they will arrive late or leave early from the office, or excuse themselves from attendance to business matters by going to school events or corporate entertainment without deducting the time from their annual leave. They will not pitch in when all hands are needed to hit a deadline. Their language and tone of voice deteriorates with subordinates. Their timekeeping is poor, arriving late for meetings or leaving early without apology. Behaviours that Casual Leaders would not tolerate of others become their right.

Training is a continuous necessity for all

Each of the armed services puts their officer cadets through weeks of training – some for nearly a whole year. Much of the training is about personal discipline, fitness, tactics or weaponry, but throughout their training there is a high emphasis on leadership traits, communication skills and effective team-working. There is particular emphasis on developing situational awareness so that leaders achieve goals without resorting to lethal force until it is a last resort.

Even after successful graduation to the officer corps, there is further training throughout their career in various specialisms. The armed services acknowledge that challenges and resources evolve, so knowledge and flexibility are prerequisites of effectiveness.

I am unaware of many organisations that invest in training of leadership skills. Even for sales or operations departments, with high numbers of employees and a need for effective people-management, training concentrates much more on administration requirements, employment law and tribunals rather that effective recruitment or motivational techniques. In fact I would go further and say that training of any kind has been viewed as a cost rather than an investment; over the years I have seen this budget savaged and treated as a luxury rather than a necessity.

It defies belief that in an ever more complicated and technology-driven world, organisations do not see the absolute need for training best practice in competencies or in how to maximise the talent and potential of the people they employ to deliver competitive advantage and excellence of results. And yet I have worked in organisations where training budgets did not exist, and employees had not been on any form of training in years. Even when I put training in place, no one had sufficient curiosity to challenge why or what the training was in. Whereas I think I should have been challenged on each individual's needs and whether I was selecting the most appropriate training for them.

○ **Thoroughly induce personnel into your purpose, history, heroes – and celebrate them**

Every organisation needs to forge a common bond of purpose and identity, to have a sense of tradition and examples of the past to live up to, a feeling of community and something bigger than themselves. The armed services recognise this and have built layers of customs and methods by which they deliver this knowledge and identity. They recognise and celebrate their heroes publicly.

"Whenever you see a successful business, someone once made a courageous decision." – Peter Drucker.

Every organisation has these heroes but how few recognise them? Frequently, induction into a business is ad hoc or dispensed with entirely. I have known it to be an endless round of coffee with people I never met again or needed to ever interact with in my role, and I have also experienced being shown a desk and a computer and then just abandoned to my own devices with no further direction. Only one organisation has given me a thorough introduction to the history of itself and all its products, including samples of them for me to try; this induction ended with an exam to ensure that I had gained the required knowledge to be accepted into the team. No organisation has ever pointed out their organisation's heroes to me.

An effective induction is essential to building a cohesive society. Every organisation can maintain an official history of itself for all to understand its development. Every organisation can arrange an experience of its range of products and services. An orientation that includes the following is easy enough to plan and arrange: layout of the offices: organisational protocols and procedures; meeting calendar, objectives and scheduling; key contacts required to do the job; provision of, and training in, the required equipment and software etc. And, with some planning, any organisation can create their own customs and traditions that are unique and celebrate themselves, even if it's just Founders' Day. Further than that, every organisation has heroes that exemplify the best behaviours and decision-making that they want others to aspire to. Why do they not celebrate their achievements and make them into identifiable role models?

○ **Decide, declare and deliver common values across all layers of the organisation**
Even with the challenges that come from being in the armed services, they recognise the Social Contract and their version of the Work Contract. They ensure mutual respect and dignity are preserved. They build bonds of trust to execute teamwork effectively and efficiently. And they hold ALL, irrespective of rank, to these codes of behaviour. Some organisations I know do not have a declared set of values expected of their society of employees, while for others it was just a statement or a tick-box exercise on the annual appraisal or satisfaction survey – just acknowledging you knew what the values were and not exploring if you or your colleagues lived up to them.

For me, values are essential and indispensable. They set down a code of behaviour that you are going to be held to and that you can expect from all your colleagues including your superiors. This removes doubt or assumption, ensuring there is a level playing field to expedite personal performance, enhance co-operation and teamwork, and is the foundation for a purposeful and high-performing organisation. More on this in the next chapter!

○ **Look after the well-being of the people who report into you.**
"Unselfishness, as far as you are concerned means simply this – you will put first the honour and interests of your

country and your regiment; next you will put the safety, well-being and comfort of your men; and last – and last all the time – you will put your own safety, your own comfort." – Field Marshall Sir Bill Slim, legendary British military commander.

The US Marines explicitly talk about concern for others and concern for each other in their values. While there is clearly an expectation of personal responsibility and adult behaviours, each US Marine is reminded of their mutual dependency.

The British armed services do not specifically reference well-being in their values but it is core to the definition of the role of their leaders. In fact, the actual job profile of any of the Operational Officers for the Army, Navy and Air Force includes two direct statements on the welfare of the unit of command. It is included in the definition of the role: "Your responsibilities cover the training, fitness, operational effectiveness and welfare of everyone in the unit, so that they reach and maintain a high level of competence and readiness." And it is in the first line of general duties as part of the list of responsibilities too: "taking responsibility for the welfare, morale and motivation of subordinates".

This should not surprise anyone. The armed services are deployed in a variety of hazardous theatres at any given time. These include: peacekeeping roles, providing humanitarian aid, enforcing anti-terrorism measures, and combatting the international drugs trade as well as actual warfare. When on these operations they will be working in challenging environments, in difficult conditions and for long hours. It is imperative that the people they command are alert, rested and fed to maintain the highest effectiveness and that their commanders are charged with this responsibility. If personnel know that they are being cared for, it is one of the building blocks of trust.

How many other organisations recognise this duty of care? I have known many managers to take no responsibility for the welfare of the people who report into them. These Casual Leaders seemed blissfully ignorant of people under stress, being ill, working unreasonable hours and driving long distances when clearly exhausted. It baffles me how anyone can be discharging their responsibility as a leader if they have no regard for the work–life balance, general health and state of rest of their reports. It is self-evident that tired, stressed, hungry and unhealthy people do not work effectively or make good decisions. So why do so many leaders ignore their responsibility – and get away with it?

o **Impartially deliver rewards and consequences**
It is no coincidence that each of the armed services has embraced both the medal system and the ways of delivering military codes of justice. It is because they are effective and essential in delivering a healthy culture – a balance of reward/recognition on one hand against consequence/ punishment on the other. This is essential to ensure that the right behaviours are delivered and to build the right culture. And each of the armed services has taken care to make sure that both reward and consequence are seen to be dispensed impartially. They recognise that, for justice to be seen to be done, it must be executed objectively, fairly and consistently.

However, most organisations are less transparent. Traditionally, they show approval publicly through progress in title or rank only, while pay awards and bonus payments are kept confidential. I have even known organisations to single out favoured individuals for bonuses which were not qualified against the criteria or given to others – it is an arbitrary system of patronage when executed in this way, undermining morale and trust.

Few organisations seem to acknowledge that rewards can be in terms of public recognition, not just rank or pay. Occasionally, there are "Employee of the Month" declarations but these are usually not substantial and can be treated with derision. Sometimes people are put on public display at open meetings, much to their embarrassment and even leading to a backlash from envious colleagues. Few organisations have used demonstrative benefits, such as Richer Sounds and Asda, who provide luxury cars for a week in recognition of performance, and yet it would be so easy to do. Even the best car-parking spot being reserved at the front of the office or a special tie/scarf/pin badge award would start to deliver some tangible benefit and recognition to the recipient without courting embarrassment.

Further, many organisations lack courage when it comes to consequences. Many Casual Leaders are just suffered by their line managers due to their lack of appetite to confront poor behaviour or to discipline it. When line managers are like this, they are guilty of acting as Casual Leaders themselves. It's a vicious circle, with Casual Leaders creating more Casual Leaders beneath them.

I know of many people who have been "compromised" out of a business as the organisation wanted a swift resolution without embracing the costs of a tribunal or adverse publicity. This has included clear cases of fraud, theft or espionage for competitors. Paying someone off by honouring a contract they have betrayed is tantamount, in my view, to rewarding the offender. It gives entirely the wrong signal to all the employees who have not transgressed and hardly acts as a deterrent or builds towards a healthy working culture.

At other times, punishment has been different dependent on offender or disciplining manager so the fairness and impartiality of the system has been flouted. One rule for one, another rule for another. I have even known this to set precedents when more people have failed in the same behaviour at a later date – effectively redefining and weakening the desired consequence as an option.

If all employees do not see justice applied impartially within the system, the whole system starts to decay. Consistency, fairness and visibility are imperative to be effective and key to delivering trust.

Just as organisations can review their range of options to reward people, they can do so also with their range of consequences. Organisations can embrace public censure of individuals, or remove them from the organisation for breaking or failing their contract, so long as they do so in a way that that does not deny people the right to dignity and respect. And organisations should not be conducting disciplinary systems inconsistently, subjectively, furtively or secretively as if it is somehow shameful. But this does require leaders with a good moral compass and the courage to act. It can be done; the armed services do so.

THE BEST TEAM IN THE WORLD?

There are some cultures that not only produce success but have managed to sustain that performance over time. For most organisations, maintaining momentum and delivering sustainable results even in the short term is too much. What can we learn from an organisation that has performed at the highest levels, against world-class competition, and sustained their performance for decades?

The New Zealand national rugby union team is commonly called the All Blacks after their distinctive playing kit. Rugby Union is like a religion within the country and the nation identifies itself with the national team and its success. For many boys it is their childhood dream to eventually become an All Black. Their heroes are idolised; the nation rejoices with the success of the team and goes into collective mourning when they fail. Expectations are high; interest is intense; speculation on player selection, coach appointments and tactics is vocal; and there is constant pressure on the players and coaches as each performance is minutely critiqued and commented on by the press and public. No other team could have such an impact on their citizens' sense of well-being.

At the time of writing, ESPN shows the All Black all-time win percentage at 79.1%! That's right; they have won 444 of the 581 matches they have played since 1903 – and they drew a further twenty. In their 115 years of representing their country they have only lost 110 times – less than once a year on average. In comparison, Brazil, who are often considered the most successful international football team of all time, have won only 63.3% of their all-time matches.

What is even more remarkable about the All Blacks is that they have sustained this success for so many years and yet have one of the smallest populations and playing bases from which to select.

Top Tier 1 Rugby Nations	All-Time Win %	Player Base in 2018
All Blacks (NZ)	79.1%	151k
South Africa	64.7%	468k
England	58.4%	2,140k
France	56.0%	634k

The All Blacks are the only international rugby side with a winning record against every other opponent and jointly hold the record for the most consecutive test match wins for a tier-one nation. Since 1903, they have lost to only six of the nineteen nations that they have played in matches. And they have won the International Rugby World Cup three times since it was first created as a tournament in 1987.

It would be easy to assume that the All Blacks have some sort of winning formula that no one else has caught on to, and they have just stuck to it. But their success has not always been assured.

The year 1995 was pivotal in rugby union. The game went professional and attracted significant TV audiences and investment around the world. South Africa was allowed back into international games after years of exclusion due to apartheid and went onto win the Rugby World Cup. For a while it looked as if the All Blacks would adjust to this new world, supported by genuine superstar players such as Jonah Lomu. However the cracks began to appear and their previous supremacy was threatened by South Africa, Australia and France. Within a matter of years, their win percentage was looking average by their standards and in 1999 they only achieved fourth place in that year's World Cup. It was a shock to the national psyche of the entire country! The nation went through all the stages of the grief process before accepting the result: shock, denial, bargaining and anger.

ALL BLACKS RESULTS BY YEAR
(SOURCE: ESPN)

Year	Matches	Won	Lost	Draw	%
1995	12	10	2	0	83%
1996	10	9	1	0	90%
1997	12	11	0	1	92%
1999	12	9	3	0	75%
2000	10	7	3	0	70%
2001	10	8	2	0	80%
2002	11	8	2	1	73%
Total	77	62	13	2	81%

A revolution was started. The seeds of this can be seen with an initiative from retired players John Kirwan and Sean Fitzpatrick, who produced *The Black Book* in attempting to define the essential, historic culture that had brought so much success in the past. In 1999, Kirwan and Fitzpatrick were national heroes for winning the inaugural Rugby World Cup twelve years before and this book captured the collected wisdom of former players. It still informs the new culture today but it was not a magic remedy on its own. Coaches came and went; performances did not improve significantly or consistently; further World Cup success was still elusive. It was not until the appointment of a new coach, Graham Henry, in 2003 that the rigour of a new culture started to take shape. And, despite further World Cup disappointment in 2007, Henry, his coaching staff and lead players kept faith and the results came through, leading to two World Cup wins in succession.

ALL BLACKS RESULTS BY YEAR
(SOURCE: ESPN)

Year	Matches	Won	Lost	Draw	%
2003	14	12	2	0	86%
2004	11	9	2	0	82%
2005	12	11	1	0	92%
2006	13	12	1	0	92%
2007	12	10	2	0	83%
2008	15	13	2	0	87%
2009	14	10	4	0	71%
2010	14	13	1	0	93%
2011	12	10	2	0	83%
2012	14	12	1	1	86%
2013	14	14	0	0	100%
2014	14	12	1	1	86%
2015	12	11	1	0	92%
2016	14	13	1	0	93%
2017	14	11	2	1	79%
Total	**199**	**173**	**23**	**3**	**87%**

Unfortunately for their opponents, the All Blacks had not only got back to winning ways; they got better and still better. So much so that their most iconic player, Richie McCaw, who played in 148 matches between 2001 and 2015, enjoyed an all-time win percentage of 89.2%! And since the introduction of the World Rugby rankings in 2003, they have held the number one ranking longer than all other teams combined.

It is a level of sustained success that cannot be rivalled by any other team in any other sport. And clearly they have changed players and coaches over time, and had to respond to new game rules and interpretations. But they have shown that they can sustain that performance and continue to evolve their game regardless of the talent and innovation brought by other countries in the intense rivalry of international sport. So what is their secret? And what can other organisations learn from them in creating a high performance and engaged culture?

There is an aura of mystique around the All Blacks and they are not foolish enough to allow a definitive description of their methods and culture. However, there are a number of credible sources which give us a glimpse into their world. I am particularly indebted to the business consultant James Kerr, who has written a fantastic book called *Legacy* in which he analyses fifteen lessons in leadership to be learnt from the All Blacks. This should be a must-read for all businessman and people-managers! Plus other sources that include interviews of former players and Richie McCaw's own autobiography *The Real McCaw*. And there are a number of themes in the way the All Blacks have organised themselves which are consistent with previous commentary in this book.

For example, the All Blacks' "purpose" is described by McCaw as being quite simple. "Performing on the field, winning games is what the All Blacks is all about." However they recognise also that they have a wider social context within which they work. James Kerr describes their vision as ambitious: "To unite and inspire New Zealand", which is aligned to very stretching targets set by Graham Henry. "The challenge is always to improve, to always get better. Even when you are the best. Especially when you are the best."

With a clear purpose and vision, the *challenge* for each All Black and the team was defined. How did they deliver the *support*?

Graham Henry's leadership style was clearly "Authoritative". McCaw describes a typical week before a test match as "At the beginning of the week it is 80/20 coaches driving things at practice; by the end of the week it is 80/20 players as they have to drive it in the game". McCaw has a very high respect for the intelligence and analysis brought by all the coaching staff of their opponents and emerging trends in the way the game was played. But he goes on to talk about how the coaches would encourage the senior players to take responsibility for the ownership of game solutions by asking them interrogative questions – just like Jack Welch advocated at General Electric. As previously argued, this style allows greater emotional buy-in and acceptance of responsibility. Henry was clear that he wanted to pass responsibility from the coaches to the senior team and players, while not relieving himself of overall accountability. "Leaders create leaders" was his mantra. He felt that by creating ownership they would feel responsibility and trust, which allowed for autonomy of decision-making and that the players would take the initiative during the game. He was looking for individuals who would thrive on testing themselves with the challenge to succeed and the responsibility to the nation that implied.

These are "Adult" to "Adult" transactions. This "Authoritative" leadership style worked; whereas McCaw's description of the previous coaching staff was indicative of a "Coercive" leadership style, or "Critical Parent" to "Child" transactions – "Do what I tell you".

Further, Henry devolved the management authority through the squad. Leadership groups were formed under seasoned players. They were given a distinct range of responsibilities both on and off field – from leadership in the game to social organisation, community relations and sponsor appearances, through to mentoring the new, younger players. By getting the older players to groom and induct the newer players into the expectations of the All Blacks and nation, Henry was ensuring that the group as a whole felt in control and were taking responsibility for the destiny. These leadership groups took on the responsibility for key decisions, and enforcing standards and behaviour. It was a highly effective way of ensuring that the squad perpetuated any *support* given by the coaches in meeting the *challenge*. They see that leaders have to create a learning environment in which the right behaviours flourish. So they eliminate any that are resistant to change, learning or taking responsibility so that they can build the capability of those that remain or join.

Similar to the armed services analysis earlier, the All Blacks appoint players on *character*, not just *competency*. James Kerr quotes Andrew Mehrtens, one of the most talented All Blacks of the past: "If you have personal discipline in your life then you are going to be more disciplined on the field. If you're wanting guys to pull together as a team, you've got to have that. You don't want a group of individuals," and, "It's about thinking about the team's interest before yourself... if it's not good for the team, don't say it and don't do it." Kerr goes on to assert that some of the most talented rugby players in New Zealand will either never become All Blacks or will not survive in their environment. It is not just about being skilful, powerful or fit. It is about having the right work ethic; taking personal responsibility and acting with integrity; being passionate about becoming an All Black and understanding what their success means to the nation; having the self-sacrificing mindset required to improve personal performance to elite standards; having the courage to face up to the brutal contests in a high-speed collision sport; being honest about your own and your teammates' performance; and being unselfish and having an unfailing commitment to the team as a whole.

In fact, while there is no definitive description of the required characteristics to be an All Black, it is this utter commitment to the team that most commentators reaffirm. In their *Black Book*, Kirwan and Fitzpatrick state clearly that, "No one is bigger than the team"; Kerr attributes the philosophy to one borrowed from the Sydney Swans, a professional Australian rules football club – "No dickheads" – while McCaw describes it as a "prickless environment". Kerr describes this as eradicating disaffected or selfish individuals from the group of players so as to create a healthy environment.

So, the All Blacks ensured that they recruited and developed individuals that bring not just the right energy to the squad but also the right attitude. Players that managed to get through the selection criteria filter were soon found out by their peers and their coaches only to be excluded in the future. The All Blacks clearly only wanted Lineberry's definition of Players; the Walking Dead and Spectators were excluded from the outset while the Well Poisoners were ejected.

The All Blacks have a values-led culture. Brian Lochore, a former All Blacks player and coach, describes it as, "Better people make better All Blacks." There is an acknowledgement that we all have a front that we display to the world – the "false me" – but the coaches distinguish the need for absolute self-awareness – and embracing the "real me". This is about understanding and owning our own strengths and weaknesses so that we can improve. It is only from gaining this awareness that we can be authentic and therefore trustworthy. So it would be no surprise if key among the values of the All Blacks were honesty and integrity. However, they are not! As Fitzpatrick said, "You shouldn't really need to work on those, they should be a given." They are in fact part of the essential character to be considered even as a potential All Black.

Kerr reveals that Saatchi & Saatchi helped New Zealand Rugby Union to develop its brand values, which included essential values of its culture. It will be no surprise that they include teamwork and excellence as core values. Commitment is a value but is expected to an extreme – "bone deep commitment not skin-deep" is how McCaw describes it. As previously established, respect is fundamental to the Social Contract and to building effective teams and they include this as one of their values too. But perhaps the most surprising, and most compelling, of their values is humility.

Humility seems to me to be the single most differentiating value of the All Blacks and perhaps it explains why, for all their success, most rugby fans around the world are not begrudging but admire their prowess. The English are seen as unimaginative and arrogant, the French as flash and unpredictable, the Australians as cocky and brash, the South Africans as brutally powerful; and the Welsh are perceived as both poor winners and poor losers. But the All Blacks set a pinnacle of behaviour we admire; they are gracious in defeat, without whining or complaining, and there is an absence of arrogance when they win. In part it is about accepting personal responsibility for tailored training and for performance by the individual; in part it is about acknowledging the great players of the past and their achievements that the current players need to live up to, but it is also acknowledging the weight of expectations of their nation and the pressure that brings to win on every occasion. As Fitzpatrick stated in a recent documentary, "Every man and boy in New Zealand would trade places with you [a player] tomorrow". He saw it as an honour and not a job.

Having humility gives the All Blacks a vital opportunity. It allows themselves to ask the questions: "How can we improve?

How can we get better?" It helped McCaw with his captaincy too. Following the 2007 World Cup he recalls that, just because he was captain, that didn't mean he knew everything and that he was confident to be able to ask other senior players their opinions and to follow their advice. In the biopic *Chasing Great*, one of the coaches explains that the team rationalised that success is not a great teacher and that the All Blacks try to learn the lessons from their rare failures, while McCaw asks himself, "What should I have done better? Why didn't I do this?"

And it is humility that drives their thirst to learn, to improve, and to get better. This value ensures a learning culture. It prevents the complacency and arrogance that affects so many other successful organisations and which leads to their own declining performance over time.

And, as with the armed services, the All Blacks are very aware of their legacy, the success and heroes of the past, and have established a critical identity through their customs and traditions. Most rugby fans will be aware of the Haka, the Maori and Polynesian tribal challenges that the All Blacks confront their opponents with before each match. The Haka is a traditional war cry, a mixture of shouts and rhythmic chanting with co-ordinated posturing to intimidate the enemy. It is one of the greatest traditions in sport, a compelling piece of theatre for fans and widely enjoyed around the world. It gets the blood pumping and the increased flow of adrenaline required to go into battle, even if you are just a fan and watching the ritual! It has a vital purpose in uniting the team in their resolve and objective, anchoring their endeavour with the legacy of successful teams from the past, and ensuring that each player is in the moment and fully focussed on the next eighty minutes of effort.

But fans may not be aware of the ceremony that goes with the awarding of the first All Black shirt to each player, where the recipient is exhorted to leave the shirt in a better place than they inherited it – it is not good enough to be a good All Black; they must aspire to be a great All Black! Their iconic play-maker of this century and the player with the record for the most points scored, Dan Carter, confirmed the emotional impact of this ceremony in a recent documentary: "It is impressed on you that you are a caretaker of the shirt."

Each player is given the *Black Book*, which has photos of each team's strip over the last century, as well as the exhortation that they are All Blacks 24/7 and a list of the standards and team protocols such as the dress code, recovery process after a game, post-match boundaries of behaviour and the expectations of each player. Perhaps most telling is that one of the key rules is to Always Be on Time – presumably as a mark of respect to everyone else – and the players were not afraid to hold the current coach to that measure recently. But, for me, the most telling part of the book are the blank pages at the back, to remind them they are going to make their own history of the shirt, as part of the legacy of the All Blacks of the past, and within a continuous chain into the future after they have retired!

All rugby teams have their own initiation rituals, flags on the wall, anthems, caps and places-on-the-bus rights for senior players, which forges their sense of identity. However, the All Blacks have a unique tradition whenever they play Wales – as the team bus goes over the Severn Bridge to enter Wales everyone on the bus gets up and shouts, "We never lose to Wales!" How glorious to be that confident!

All of these mechanics, customs and traditions have helped the All Blacks to forge a unique and unifying identity. As previously stated, this is essential in building emotional connections between individuals and is at the core of creating an effective, positive and engaging team culture.

The All Blacks are constantly mindful of the well-being of their players. In the high-octane world of their rugby style, where players are reminded to leave all their effort out on the pitch, they get both physically and mentally exhausted. The danger is that not only will that lead to poor decision-making on the field but it can also lead to or exacerbate injuries, thus denying players the next match to play and disrupting the team.

In recent years, the Tri-Nations tournament in which the All Blacks play other southern-hemisphere sides has been expanded to include Argentina. At provincial level, their franchise teams now play in an expanded Super Rugby tournament as well, which includes international travel. And there has been demand for an expanded international fixture list to satisfy sponsors and to drive incremental revenue. All of this has drastically increased the amount of rugby played and travel away from family and friends. The new All Black coach Steve Hanson and the recently retired captain McCaw have each talked at length about the challenge of managing these workloads so that fatigue is avoided and the players are kept in good physical condition and mentally fresh. Hanson has also had to manage the normal retirement of a number of key players, following success at the 2015 Rugby World Cup, with the resultant loss of experienced senior players and the need to recharge a successful culture with younger players. Speaking in August 2017, Hanson said, "The big banana skin is nine weeks, seven tests and round the world twice with ten time changes."

Unlike most other countries, New Zealand have an established system of central contracts for All Black players. This allows the coach to exercise some degree of control over players even though they will be contracted also to Super Rugby franchises. It was Graham Henry who first started to use these contracts effectively by resting players, rotating them and negotiating recovery times with the franchise teams. And he came in for a lot of criticism for it from both fans and former All Blacks at the time. But it is a system that has allowed far greater rest periods for All Black players than other countries and the team performances has benefited for it. Not only were players kept fresher and careers extended but when injuries came along or enforced retirements occurred he was able to call on a greater pool of players who knew the systems and ethos of the team so the All Blacks could retain momentum and results. Dan Carter and Richie McCaw were even able to negotiate sabbaticals from the All Black camp to give their bodies better recovery time and return them fresh for the 2015 World Cup. But even with all this Hanson is having to consider more radical ideas to rest his players.

The recent success of the Irish national team has also been attributed to their adoption of central contracts. A former All Black, Jimmy Gopperth, in an interview in 2018 is absolutely clear that this gives the Irish and the All Blacks a significant advantage. "These guys [the Irish team] are mentally fresher for the simple reason they get longer rest periods. The All Blacks clocked off for fourteen weeks when they finished their tour in Europe in November... The upside is that because you have been able to switch off, you come back really sharp and eager to go, mentally refreshed. At Leinster you'd only see the Irish boys for say ten provincial games. That's why the Irish teams are top of the European pile at the moment." He went on then to compare the demands on an England player, who might have a continuous season for most of the year with demands from the Six Nations championship, Premiership Club league matches, Champions Cup, international summer tour and finally the World Cup in 2019. "Good luck with that."

All organisations are required by UK law to ensure the physical safety of their workforce. But how many organisations actually ensure that their workforce is not physically exhausted by the demands on them? And how many organisations say that they truthfully are mindful of their employees' mental health and mental freshness?

There is one process by which the All Blacks are distinctly different to any organisation I have worked with commercially. The coaching team's performance is reviewed annually.

In his autobiography, McCaw reveals that the coaching staff are held fully accountable on an annual basis. Every year the All Black coaches have to go through a 360-degree, anonymous online review system. Players, co-coaches, staff, management and some media and sponsors all complete a series of questions on their performance. This is accountability in action and ensures that even those at the top have an impartial feedback mechanism that raises their self-awareness on impact and behaviour. The parallel commercially would be for the CEO and executive directors to be appraised by the chairman and non-executive directors with input from all stakeholders including their own management teams. That would be revolutionary!

As you can see, there are many parallel lessons that can be drawn from both the armed services and the All Blacks to inform other organisations on how to create a healthy, engaged culture. The All Black experience shows that, even with phenomenal success behind you, the culture cannot be taken for granted. The world moves on; challenges change; new personnel and systems force you to constantly adapt and evolve. The real enemy is complacency and it is hard work to define and sustain a high-performance environment no matter who you are and what legacy you have inherited. But the All Blacks have shown also that it can be done – it requires commitment, ruthless attention to detail and constant monitoring of progress. And the results can also be enjoyable.

All of this is evident to anyone who takes the time to review them. Not long ago I led a strategy session for the heads of department of a medium-sized business. Between the five of them, they managed a total of 100 employees and contractors, so effective leadership and teamwork was a core opportunity for them. I planned to review James Kerr's observations on the leadership lessons of the All Blacks with them within the session and we started with a ten-minute video of the highlights of their recent performances. Only one of the group was a rugby fan and their collective knowledge was limited. However by the end everyone was amazed, captivated and enthusiastic. One lady from South America had never heard of the All Blacks before, or seen the game played, but was enthralled by the passion of the Haka and the skill of the team.

I asked them to list their observations from the film before we reviewed the book. Here are some of the descriptions they used:

Connection with the fans; fun; celebration; support; speed; joy; humility; create opportunity; focus; work ethic; friendship; trust; power; leadership; brilliant at the basics; complimentary skills; multi-skilled; momentum; well drilled; execution; ruthless; ambitious; teamwork; composure; engaged.

The last words in this chapter should come from a man who was there and a fundamental part of that All Black evolution. Richie McCaw was already an All Black when Graham Henry was appointed as a coach. And his career extended beyond that of Henry's tenure as coach. He is not only the most capped international player but also the most capped All Black captain and the only captain to have retained the World Cup title in successive tournaments. He is frequently described as the greatest All Black in history and proposed as the best rugby player ever. What was his verdict?

"He [Graham Henry] created an environment that I and the others bought into, and he was determined to do everything we could every day to get the results we desired." It's a glowing reference for a leader and I wonder how many CEOs or board members would receive praise like that?

EIGHTEEN MEASURES TO CREATE AN ENGAGED CULTURE

What gets measured gets improved. At the start of this section, I set out that the CEO is accountable, and the board were responsible, for creating an effective culture in their organisation. Casual Leaders can only exist if the board allows them, or if the directors are themselves Casual Leaders and providing a poor role model to the rest of the organisation.

The research quoted shows that many businesses do not take this responsibility as seriously as they should: not measuring what the actual culture is; not knowing what it should be; having no measurement in place; and not finding the time to discuss it. And yet I have shown other organisations do take it seriously and it does bring rewards in performance.

I have argued that an "engaged" culture establishes trust, and creates effective teamwork. It ensures information-sharing is optimised and co-operation is maximised but still requires effective processes to be efficient. And I am not the only commentator to argue this. In his book *Trust Works*, Ken Blanchard sets out that there are a number of unconscious behaviours which inhibit trust. He believes that we have to be aware of, and develop, four key behaviours that address the core issues behind poor morale, fractured relationships, ineffective transactions and dysfunctional leadership to create an organisation with an engaged health state. He summarises it by proposing a simple ABCD model which I have illustrated below.

KEN BLANCHARD'S ABCD ON HOW TO BUILD TRUST

ABLE (demonstrate competence)	BELIEVABLE (act with integrity)
Get quality results Resolve problems Develop skills Be good at what you do Get experience Use your skills to assist others	Keep confidences Admit when you are wrong Be honest Don't talk behind backs Be sincere Be non-judgemental Show respect
CONNECTED (care about others)	DEPENDABLE (maintain reliability)
Listen well Praise others Show interest in others Work well with others Show empathy for others Ask for input	Do what you say you will do Be timely Be responsive Be organised Be accountable Follow up Be consistent

The recurring themes in this book are obvious in Blanchard's model. Do not concentrate on competencies alone, even though they are important of course. Do ensure that the right values are in place as they are the appropriate behaviours to create a reasonable and engaged society or culture. And do develop and demonstrate self-awareness, plus emotional and social intelligence, within the leadership and through the workforce.

So what are the practical measures that the CEO, board and other leaders can put in place within an organisation to create this engaged culture? Below is my opinion. It is not meant to be a definitive list but the bare minimum required to create a fair, productive society and an engaged culture in any organisation. Some of these recommendations are well known as best practice, while some are just common sense, and you may wonder why I have bothered to include them. Sadly, the evidence I have seen is that standards have slipped over many years and these actions either no longer exist, or have become a slipshod process and are not effectively enforced. You may find other recommendations are more radical!

1 **Have a dedicated HR professional as a director on the board**
You might think this would be standard practice in any company of a decent size. In practice I have known companies with over 50,000 employees with no HR director at all! Even when one exists it is often combined with another remit (e.g. legal secretary) and the individual is not a trained professional in human resources. None of these examples shows a serious intent by the organisation to take people seriously as an asset or to maximise the talent and potential of their employees.

Attitudes to HR have been disappointing at times. I have heard them referred to as "sales prevention officers" or "the enemy within" by board directors and even "the state police" by employees. Personally I think this has something to do with the traditional perception that HR has a narrow role: enforcing legal compliance; managing industrial action and tribunals; disciplinary processing; administration of payroll and benefits; recruiting; writing the employee handbook, etc. Restricted to this remit, human resources are seen as paperwork creators and behavioural police – "HR says NO!" The board have treated the function as solely there to meet the needs of management and particularly for controlling costs or complaints, while employees have resented and distrusted HR for doing so. For example, training budgets have been successively reduced in every year of the last three decades I have worked, frustrating employees who needed new skills or other development.

However, there is a much wider strategic opportunity for a modern HR function. If the board chooses, the HR remit can include: thorough on-boarding of new employees; leadership training; performance development; succession-planning; cultural engagement policies; empowerment policies through increased responsibility; talent management; and being the primary function for change management. To do so though requires real change in attitude by the CEO and board. People have to be seen as an essential asset to be developed and motivated not just managed. Talent has to be identified, recruited and nurtured by the organisation. Casual Leaders have to be "outed" and removed if necessary. The training budget cannot be seen just as a cost but should be viewed as a strategic investment and a lever to build capability, engagement, team-working and skill thresholds. In other words the CEO has to put people as a priority on her/his agenda; and the board has to start being proactive rather than reactive. A dedicated HR professional on the board ensures that this can happen.

2 **Put an ARCI model in place across the entire organisation**
I believe this to be the most essential and first step in structuring effective, engaging policies.

An ARCI model is a simple matrix that is used to describe the responsibilities of various roles in achieving progress or delivery of an organisation's key objectives. It can be applied to every single part of an organisation and can even capture all the key metrics that make up an organisation's profit and loss account – so should not just be consigned to projects alone.

The model shows: who is **Accountable** for a decision/process/key deliverable or performance indicator; who is **Responsible** for actually making it happen; who needs to be **Consulted** within the process, and who needs to be **Informed** that it is taking place.

I have worked in two organisations in which this has been an established matrix for decision-making – they have had clearly better cultural health states than any of the organisations in which the model was absent. In essence it removes any uncertainty in the roles and responsibilities across departments, or of individuals, and effectively delegates the authority and remit for decision-making. It cuts out turf wars between departments and individuals; it ensures collaboration and co-operation; it means that communication is enhanced and it enforces efficiency of process. There is high visibility for all, with recognition of good execution and nowhere to hide in the event of failure or poor performance.

In contrast, those organisations that have not had an ARCI model in place have demonstrated inefficiency and confusion. At their worst, leadership and decision-making has been dysfunctional allowing chaotic or toxic cultures to develop.

In those organisations in which the ARCI model has been absent, I have seen even key decisions such as pricing having no overall owner and therefore no strategy or concerted thought applied to it. So the biggest and clumsiest lever to create or destroy sales and profit has been directionless, ignored the competitor context or consumers' perceptions, and become subject to anyone's influence no matter how badly thought through and with no consequences for decision-making. Similarly I have seen sales departments who have chased orders, but not been held accountable for the discounts they have promised to suppliers, and destroying the profitability of products or services. Or construction departments who have decided they have authority over the store layout without consulting operators or training and impeding service efficiency or processes; or assuming they had authority for store design rather than marketing and creating alien, unattractive environments for the customer to experience.

It does require a painstaking approach to capture all the key processes and performance metrics for an ARCI model to work. This is an unavoidable investment of time and discussion up front but reaps enormous rewards in efficiency and effective teamwork later. It has the benefit also of preventing the CEO from adopting a predominantly Coercive or Pacesetting leadership style. As previously argued, many appear to think they are "accountable" (or the "final approving authority") for every single decision and action taken, and for every deliverable on the P&L, instead of effectively delegating authority. This is the reason why CEOs are not focussed on their key role in defining strategy, managing stakeholders, setting the annual plan and budget, measuring progress of it, marshalling resource for short and long term (including management and employees), and delivering an engaged culture.

ARCI MODEL FOR DECISION-MAKING AND ACTION-TAKING

Accountable	Only one person can be the final decision maker and ultimate owner for the completion of each task or deliverable.
(also known as: Final Approving Authority or Approver):	The Accountable is the person who must sign off and approve the work that the Responsible provides. Therefore, the Responsible reports into him/her.
Responsible	This can one or more people who are held Responsible for the implementation of the task and achievement of the deliverable.
Consulted	These are the people whose opinions are needed; and with whom there is two-way communication before the decision is taken. Typically the decision or work being progressed directly affects their own area of work.
Informed	These people are not directly impacted by the decisions being progressed nor achievement of the task or deliverable. However they need to be kept up-to-date; this is only one-way communication after the decision or action has been taken.

3   **Maintain and publish the organisation's organogram**
The ARCI model allows full visibility of where manpower should be invested, in what quantities and with what level of experience.

Bizarrely, I have found a number of organisations do not draw up a diagram that shows the structure of how they are organised, and the relationships and relative grades of its departments and jobs. This is called an organisational chart or "organogram". Sometimes, even if they do have an organogram, some organisations do not publish it internally or allow visibility across the organisation.

There are clear benefits to be found in planning short- and long-term resources through organograms as it allows a helicopter view of resource and an objective assessment of resource allocation. If visible to all, it facilitates greater teamwork, co-operation, information-sharing and communication. A further benefit is that it also allows employees a broader understanding of the organisation and shows how they can develop their career.

If an organisation cannot or will not express resource in this way, I would seriously doubt the ability of the CEO to execute one of his/her main objectives – efficient resource allocation.

4   **Maintain an equitable salary band and rewards structure**
The organogram determines how many people are required and at what grade or level of experience. It shows the leadership structure across an organisation and the number of people that each manager is responsible for in their role.

The next step is to ensure broad equity of reward, in terms of salary and other benefits, across the organisation. This is essential to deliver a fair society.

Often I have found that there has been no attempt to ensure equity between departments on either role definition, responsibility or reward. I have even found individuals on higher salary and rewards packages than the management grades above them within the same teams. This implied that increased responsibility and impact warranted less reward!

I have seen new area managers secure higher grades and rewards, when only responsible for twenty stores, than seasoned heads of department who directly impacted the performance of 500 stores and the whole company P&L. This was not justified by market rates; he who shouts loudest, it seems!

On one occasion I greeted a colleague on the same grade by saying it was bonus week, not realising he was not included in that scheme. He resigned in disgust at the lack of fairness.

Any organisation that does not believe that employees talk amongst themselves, and broadly understand each other's salary and bonus, is sadly mistaken. Any inequity and unfairness will be discovered with repercussions on morale and staff retention. While employees can accept that there will always be salary bands within each grade, to reflect broader experience or nuances of responsibility, they will rightly challenge unfairness. And this is entirely in the board's gift when deciding what sort of society or culture they are trying to create.

For tangible equity, I have found that organisations that use the Hay Job Evaluation scoring system, or similar, have delivered fairer cultures. This attempts to score the value, impact and responsibility of widely different roles (e.g. research scientist vs sales representative) to establish a job grade for each; and then ensure that job grades have distinct steps of reward between them to reflect the additional responsibility that comes with higher grades. The methodology delivers a framework where rewards and responsibility are broadly equitable across the organisation. NB This still has to be tempered by market rates for certain roles.

5   **Give everyone a written job description**

It sounds ridiculous but I have found that a number of organisations have failed to tell individuals what the remit, authority limits and expectations are of their role. I have found that often I have not had a job description myself.

Everywhere I have worked captures the limits for discretionary expenditure or approving expenses but often they fail to put the same rigour into authority on decision-making or behaviours required in the role. Where job descriptions have existed, I have found that they are frequently out of date or inconsistent from one individual to another depending on who created them.

An ARCI model ensures that everyone knows with whom and which department authority exists but this should be cascaded and caught within each individual's job description too. It protects both the organisation and the individual and should be their right alongside their work contract.

It need not be exhaustive, although at the extreme I have seen job descriptions that are so detailed they lack impact! At the minimum the job description should:

o   express the organisation's purpose;
o   define the remit of the relevant department;
o   confirm the job title and grade of the individual;
o   detail the key deliverables of the role using action words (i.e. responsible for gross profit; consulted on promotions etc.);
o   set out the resource they are responsible for (e.g. people and budgets); and
o   set out the values or behaviours expected (of their grade and as a member of the organisation).

6 **Define the values or behaviours expected of everyone in the organisation**

If you do not define the behaviours you expect, do not be surprised when you do not get them! You have no right to be disappointed or hold people to a standard that you could not be bothered to state.

Not everyone has had the same education; not everyone has been brought up on the same definition of good and bad; different cultures, religions and families will have different expectations of social norms and good citizenship. If you do not clearly state expectations, you are just working from a presumption and you would not do that in any other situation at work.

In the next section we will explore how to determine the appropriate values for any organisation but the overwhelming evidence presented shows that these are required to deliver an engaged culture.

In practice I have found a number of organisations do not have a declared set of values or just pay them lip service. For me, this is in itself Casual Leadership. I believe that appropriate social behaviours are not only essential to create an engaged culture but they must be taken seriously and become part of the DNA of an organisation.

The best organisation I worked for not only had a declared set of standards (they called them competencies) but also role-modelled them effectively from top to bottom of the structure. They were included in the six-monthly appraisal of each employee and were an integral part of the feedback to each individual. Further, the list of competencies was expanded as the roles increased in seniority in the organisation and were graded within a declared structure so that feedback was specific on what was expected and what was being evidenced.

Conversely, I know of several organisations that had a lacklustre approach. Some did not have a declared set of values or behaviours at all. One organisation confined the communication of them to "inspirational" posters on the wall, illustrated with people who were supposed to be role models but who in practice had either left the business (in some cases had been fired) or who clearly did not exhibit the behaviours illustrated. A further organisation declared their values and included them in their appraisals as a tick-box exercise but the values were not role-modelled even by the board directors.

Values are vitally important. They can shape the fairness and also the effectiveness of the culture. They should be role-modelled at the top and measured for all. The greater the seniority of the post, the more exacting the expectations of the individual should be. If chosen wisely and enforced, values help deliver the highest levels of trust and effective teamwork within an organisation. They should become a meaningful conversation in recruitment, feedback to employees and, if necessary, exiting of individuals from an organisation. They must never be a paper exercise or tick-box process.

For me, values should be expressed consistently alongside the organisation's purpose, i.e. "This is what we are trying to do and this is the way we behave in achieving that objective." The statement of the organisation's values should be included within the annual report; on the internal walls of the buildings; in the appraisal system; within the training programmes and be a fundamental part of the recruitment process. And they must be applied within the disciplinary process with consequences for not role-modelling them. Just like the All Blacks, no one is more important than the team and the disaffected or unable need to be removed for the benefit of the team. It is with this rigour only that an effective and an engaged culture can be developed, brought to life and allowed to thrive.

7   **Introduce a stakeholder survey of the board of directors**
    There is no reason why a stakeholder survey could not be
    put in place to help measure the perceptions and culture of
    an organisation, and measure the effectiveness of the CEO
    and board.

    This would enable a 360-degree feedback mechanism
    similar to that which the All Black coaches get annually.
    It could become part of a balanced scorecard for positive
    progression of the organisation alongside the key financial
    measures of the annual plan.

    The survey participants could include managers,
    suppliers, analysts, bankers and shareholders. It could
    include questions on commitment to the organisation's
    purpose; role-modelling of the organisation's values;
    transparency, honesty, and timeliness of communication;
    comparison to competitors; personal transactions at
    differing levels or departments within the organisation (e.g.
    sales, service delivery, consumer complaints etc.); and, most
    importantly, trustworthiness (I shall explore this latter point
    further in the book).

    The survey results could be combined to create a
    balanced scorecard with other key metrics from: the P&L
    for delivery against the annual plan; customers measured
    through research and other mechanisms (trust, honesty,
    efficiency, quality, friendliness, value for money, etc.); and
    the employee engagement survey (role-modelling of values,
    communication, training, etc.).

    The benefit would be heightened self-awareness and
    an objective, all-round assessment of the organisation and
    the board's effectiveness. Too often I have found that the
    board lacks insight into its own impact and influence. There
    seems to be a prevailing attitude from directors that they
    are above reproach now. "We have made it so we must
    be good at what we do. It's everyone else that needs to be

managed and taught how to behave." A stakeholder survey could well inject some humility and accountability into that assumption.

8 Make the employee engagement survey an effective measurement tool of the culture

Many companies already use an employee engagement survey as recommended by the Financial Reporting Council.

In principle, an employee engagement survey can be a vital tool for an organisation. In theory it measures how valued employees feel; how involved/engaged/motivated they are; how enthusiastic they are about the work/ product/organisation. In practice, the frequency or even existence of employee engagement surveys are under threat from remorseless cost-cutting. And the results are often ambiguous or ignored. For instance, I am unaware of any director who has had a target to achieve a certain threshold score, and often the surveys were never presented or debated even in individual appraisals. More often than not, I have found employees have become disenchanted in these surveys, leading to low participation rates and cynical views that no action would result in any case. Apart from being ignored, these surveys are often open to abuse and manipulation by Casual Leaders, as I have described earlier in the book.

There are many types of employee engagement survey and they are frequently broken down into broad areas of feedback, e.g. leadership, enablement, alignment and development. Many questions can be quite broad on company vision, communication, knowing objectives, pride in the company, receiving recognition or likelihood to stay with the organisation. However, I have often found the surveys less than instructive or specific in critiquing leadership, and I have not seen any that feed back effectively on values, trust, empowerment, teamwork, information-sharing, co-operation, personal development and training.

For example, I think it would improve most surveys if separate feedback on the CEO, the board, individual department directors and immediate line managers against the declared values of the organisation were included. This would raise self-awareness, address development or image-correction needs, and expose Casual Leaders. It would also allow the board to benchmark current culture, measure progress toward the desired culture and put personal development plans in place for individuals.

Similarly, simple questions could identify other frustrations that hold back the development of an "engaged" culture. For example, survey feedback on approachability of senior leaders; effective team-working across departments; ease of access, speed of response and accuracy of information; efficiency of processes; clarity of authority to make decisions; levels of bureaucracy or counter-signatures imposed on decisions; suitability of equipment for purpose; accessibility of training; frequency and quality of contact with immediate line manager, levels of trust across the organisation etc.

There is no doubt in my mind that an employee engagement survey could be a force for good and for improvement. But I have also held the view that "you are employed, you should be engaged!" So how do I make sense of these contrary views? It appears to me that most people start a job as very much engaged; they only become disengaged by how they are led and how they are treated. They become disengaged by Casual Leaders! If a company is going to go to the expense of an engagement survey but not asking for penetrative feedback and is not taking action in any case, it is the height of Casual Leadership from the top of an organisation. My solution is to ask for critical feedback which informs the board on the state of the current culture, and it is then for the board to take decisive action in order to move to the desired culture.

9 **Make the appraisal system transparent, instructive and worthwhile**
In theory, many organisations have an established appraisal or performance review system in place. In practice, it is often abused or ignored through inadequate policing, even by directors themselves.

I know one local market CEO who never got an appraisal from the global director he reported into for seven years. And some departments excuse themselves completely as in the case of an operator on secondment to me who had never had structured feedback in ten years within an otherwise highly professional and compliant organisation. Looking back through my own appraisals, I can clearly see a lack of accuracy, fairness, effort, relevance or even interest from my own line managers to me. (However, one senior manager did tell me how disappointed she was that I was a smoker, and one CEO advised me to wear a nicer watch if I wanted to be considered for promotion. Feedback is a gift.)

No one enjoys the appraisal process, neither the manager giving it nor the recipient of the feedback. It can be emotionally uncomfortable, feels intrusive, often becomes time-consuming, and is sometimes irrelevant. Even when an appraisal is carried out, it can often be a lacklustre effort by both parties with little attention given to the quality of the feedback or the resulting action list. When all of this happens, it is yet another example of Casual Leaders at work.

For me, the appraisal system is a right for the employee. It can be immensely positive as an experience for them and it is an essential process to enable feedback and personal development for them to achieve their potential. Time should be taken by both parties to ensure that the appraisal is accurate, fair, helpful and worthwhile. Not giving the appraisal an appropriate amount of time and effort is as bad as not doing it at all.

In a perfect world, an appraisal would include 360-degree feedback but this is fraught with difficulty in practice. One company that tried to include this ended up with a system of 180-degree feedback, e.g. "I think you are shit and my mates at the same level agree with me." At another company, I used to routinely ask for feedback on my direct reports from key contacts in other departments to include in appraisals; I never got any response in ten years and my request was never reciprocated.

In my opinion, the appraisal system can be relatively simple but made more effective if it includes the following elements:

- Name, title, job grade, date of review.
- Progress on key deliverables and bonus potential if applicable.
- Feedback on values displayed, with 360-degree input if possible.
- Career aspirations in short and medium term to cover the next four years.
- Training undertaken and further development needs identified with a timing plan.
- Leadership challenges and development of direct reports.
- Start/stop/continue commentary on behaviours from appraiser to appraisee.
- Start/stop/continue commentary from appraisee to appraiser.
- Signature to show agreement of commentary by appraisee.
- Counter signature of appraiser and his own line manager.

This methodology ensures objective and structured feedback with transparency. It insists on an adult-to-adult transaction between manager and employee. It eradicates Casual Leadership traits, and it gives visibility for progression of development and career-aspiration for the individual while facilitating succession-planning for the organisation. It's a win–win.

10 **Ensure training budgets and courses are fit for purpose**
I have observed that training budgets have been reduced for a number of years, mostly because they have been seen as a cost rather than an investment. These budgets are at such low levels now that frequently they are no longer fit for purpose and people are not even being trained in the competencies to use the equipment they have been provided with. Recently, I have found employees that were mystified by basic Microsoft packages such as Excel or Word, yet had the latest versions of the software on their PCs. And I have found sophisticated analytical software with no one trained in how to exploit its potential to analyse data or even how to access the raw data in the first place.

Of course, sometimes it is the equipment or software that is out of date but it is usually missing skills and competencies. It's tempting to blame the accountants as they approach the budgets in different ways. Equipment is a capital budget which can be written down in the accounts against tax, and depreciated over years, while training is often a revenue budget with direct impact on the current P&L account. However, the truth is that this is the responsibility of the board and not finance.

Sometimes training can have unforeseen consequences too. I know many colleagues who attended company-approved courses on best practice only to become highly cynical and disillusioned as their own senior management persisted in some of the worst practice behaviours. I wonder how many directors or managers have adequately reviewed the training they are providing, if they provide any at all?

11 And introduce leadership training!

Chris Bryant, MP for Rhondda since 2001, was interviewed by BBC Breakfast News on 17th October 2018 regarding the allegations of abuse, bullying and harassment within the Houses of Parliament. Even the presiding officer of Parliament, the Speaker of the House, had been accused. Mr Bryant recalled witnessing many cases of bullying throughout his career, in and outside of Parliament. He thought it was a widespread issue and that often the abuser was unaware of how they behaved; that they even justified their behaviour as they had been nice on other occasions. He called for leadership training for all MPs as none of them had received any and he thought such training was imperative to improve the way that employees were being treated.

Of course it might be that not all MPs are actually of good character. Perhaps some of them are not good role models because they have low self-awareness, or do not understand the impulses behind their own behaviour. Perhaps some have poor social awareness or are not even in an "adult" mindset – certainly some of the bickering and jeering during parliamentary debates seem like they are more suited to the playground! Dare I say it? Perhaps not all MPs are selflessly motivated by universalism and benevolence to really be a servant to the people of the country. Instead some seem to be vainglorious, wanting power or its trappings, and potentially even have narcissistic personality traits. Maybe that is why so many are accused of being Casual Leaders? But let's give them the benefit of the doubt and training in leadership would certainly not make things worse.

This is an issue that is right at the heart of many organisations. Casual Leaders; casual behaviour; casual abuse of both the Social and Work Contracts. Politicians do not enjoy a reputation for straight talking but if even they can be honest enough to own up to it as an issue, why cannot other organisations?

Leadership skills can be trained but that won't make you a leader. A leader comes from character, from a deeply held set of beliefs that make values an instinctive behaviour, a moral compass that is evident in all they do. Without this in place, Casual Leaders will be found throughout the organisation. Of course the CEO or members of the board might well be Casual Leaders themselves. And certainly, Casual Leaders cannot exist beneath them in the hierarchy of an organisation without the board being casual in not rooting them out. But the board cannot be everywhere, all the time.

It seems to me that if an organisation really wants to achieve an engaged culture it would not just rely on declaring values and role-modelling them from the top. Certainly the armed services take a different view; they spend considerable time in selecting the right candidates for their character – AND THEN TRAIN THEM IN LEADERSHIP. They do not leave it to chance and peer pressure.

There are probably a number of providers with suitable courses already able to supply organisations with leadership training. If not, there is certainly a market gap to be filled. I may be biased but I think buying this book and forcing leaders to read it would be a really good start. Unsurprisingly, I believe any suitable training courses would concentrate at minimum on the following themes from the book:

- Developing self-awareness.
- Educating on emotional and social intelligence, particularly humility, empathy and sensitivity to others.
- Understanding their duty is to role-model appropriate behaviours.
- Respecting the Social and Work Contracts.
- Exploring transactional analysis and in particular adult-to-adult transactions.
- Identifying their own core motivations.
- Developing an ethos that incorporates both support and challenge.
- Role-playing the pitfalls of the Karpman Triangle vs the Winner's Triangle in terms of caring for people while helping them reach their potential.
- Securing commitment to values and role-modelling them.
- Exploring Goleman's six leadership styles and developing a breadth of technique to employ more than one.
- Educating on constructive criticism techniques and how to handle confrontation (more on this in the next section).
- Improve all-round communication skills

If all people-managers within an organisation were aware of the same agenda on leadership, and could see it role-modelled from the top, momentum would soon be gained in delivering an engaged culture.

12 Recruit on character and values. Don't impose values later on people who may not be capable

You might think this would be self-evident and a process that is already followed. That would make sense. However, I am unaware of any organisation that has set out explicitly to recruit people who believe in and display the values desired in the organisation. In my experience, most interviews and screening measures are around competencies, with a subjective and shallow assessment of a candidate's motivations and core social beliefs. There are no instructions to recruit on values. There are no minimal scores or benchmarks. There is no guidance on how to interview for or how to test behaviours.

If someone is an introvert and a loner, they will not be able to respond to an organisational value for teamwork just because you tell them retrospectively. Similarly, if a core value is creativity or innovation there are people who would struggle to display these behaviours adequately. Someone who is shy and detests confrontation will be less able to show values of courage and conviction in pushing ideas forward in an organisation that wants these behaviours. So it must make sense to explicitly recruit people who already display and are committed to the values that the organisation desires to have.

And check their CV and references thoroughly before you let them into your organisation. Over the years these checks seem to have been dispensed with or seen as a tick-box exercise. I have found colleagues who have forged degree certificates, who have claimed achievements of other people as their own, who have been fired for dishonesty or theft, who have claimed higher positions or authority or salary than they have ever earned. Once I even picked up a CV to find the candidate claimed to have had ownership of a project I had delivered in another company. Surely, if someone is going to lie or cheat to gain employment, that is a warning signal that you should not include them in your society?

13 And exit people from the organisation that cannot deliver the values

This may seem harsh. There are people who may have the right skills or competencies and deliver adequate results but do not behave in the way the organisation has determined.

If they are doing all other aspects of their role, fulfilling their contract and are not breaking the law, how can I justify recommending that they are exited from the organisation?

I have come to this conclusion from many years of experience. The organisation has a right to determine how it wants to do its business and also to assess who they are employing in doing it. There will always be square pegs and round holes, i.e. there are some people who cannot or will not behave in the way that the organisation wants.

For those that cannot conform, it may not even be their fault and in different organisational cultures they could be more suitable. It could be that their personality and character just do not fit with the culture that is required for a particular organisation, e.g. if teamwork and co-operation are highly prized then loners cannot meet the requirements.

Of highest importance, Casual Leaders should be identified and addressed as soon as possible. Their effect on everyone else is magnified because of their status, higher profile and influence. If the leadership cadre is not made up of positive role models and Lineberry's Players, all other actions on the culture will be frustrated. And yet Casual Leaders persist and often at the highest levels of an organisation where CEOs are reluctant to act against them. I know of one CEO who was approached by a director to ask if he was aware of the impact another director was having on morale. After receiving several complaints from his own managers and having confronted his colleague directly but failing to get him to change his behaviour, the director reached out to the CEO as a last resort. The CEO replied, "You cannot tell me any more than I know. I have a queue of people complaining about him. But I would rather he was in my tent pissing out than outside the tent pissing in." It was a completely inadequate response and missed the point. The director in question was in the tent and pissing on everyone and everything inside it! But the CEO was not prepared to tell him to stop pissing or piss off. It was a cop-out. The CEO's response could only have made any sort of sense if the director was uniquely capable or his inside knowledge would have been a gift to a competitor if recruited by them. Neither was true... and, even if it had been, it would not have excused his behaviours, nor the CEO's failure to address them robustly.

Some people just *will not* conform to the social norms of a culture even if coached or disciplined. It may well be because they are suffering from a personality disorder (as discussed earlier) or under the influence of some form of addiction or other health issue. However, it is just as likely that they have been the victim of Casual Leader behaviours and retreated into Lineberry's negative typologies. After all, no one started out with the intent to be like this.

Remember, it has been estimated that typically only 14% of an organisation is made up of Players, while 39% are Well Poisoners. Identify who these people are. If they are Well Poisoners and cannot change their attitude then get rid of them no matter how competent they are. Their toxic behaviour will be infecting others and increasing the cultural problems. They will be creating more Casual Leaders and more Well Poisoners or destroying the energy of others.

There is a greater prospect for improvement with the other types of people identified by Lineberry. If they are Spectators, encourage them to bring energy by delegating authority, giving them responsibility and rewards for initiative. If they are the Walking Dead, build their confidence, and build their capability through skills training and putting them in positions of responsibility.

At some stage an organisation has to recognise that some of these people are a lost cause; they cannot be reformed and cannot change. They will continue to resist or disrupt the organisation, either passively or actively, to the detriment of everyone else. It seems to me to be an adult and responsible action to identify and then exit these people. They cannot be happy and fulfilled, and they will distract everyone else.

I know a number of organisations that have not had the courage to behave in this way. They have allowed disaffected people to continue employment and ignored their impact on others. It has left me baffled. Organisations do not hesitate from exiting employees that break their contract (e.g. by stealing), or who have a different skill set than the organisation needs now, or even for "their face no longer fits" (i.e. they argued with their boss). So why not get rid of employees that do not pull their weight in creating an "engaged" culture? Even employees that have been proven to be dishonest, or to be shirking, or even incompetent have been tolerated and kept in place. In my opinion this is Casual Leadership. Everyone else in the team has had to pick up the other person's share of work while the culprit continues to enjoy all the benefits of employment that they have. It is unfair and it rots the culture from the inside. It erodes respect for the leaders, it becomes a source of discontent for the able and it sets a poor example for the weak to follow.

14 Exit people in the right way

Some people decide to work for someone else. Others have been found to have redundant skills for the future needs of the organisation and are told to leave. Some may have been encouraged to go as their behaviour was fine but their performance was not up to standard. And yet others may have been fired, for incompetence or for breaching the rules of their work contract, and told to go. That's life. It is inevitable that there will be changes in personnel in any organisation and in some ways that is healthy.

However, I have often seen people treated badly when this happens. And that is always unhealthy for individuals and for the culture of the organisation.

Employment is a voluntary arrangement and people can always choose to work for someone else. Perhaps they want a change of marketplace, or it is a promotion, or they think there will be greater development opportunities elsewhere, or it could even be that they just want an easier commute to work. And, yet, I have seen managers react as if they were being personally rejected. Sometimes their behaviours have been churlish or even rude. At other times, I have seen the exit process made as difficult and as hostile as possible when someone chooses to go to a competitor – as if it was an act of treason and personal disloyalty. Once, I discovered that a whole department had been made redundant secretly when I found my phone calls were no longer being answered – no announcement, no explanation, no farewell to respected colleagues. I still cannot understand the reason it was treated so furtively, as if it was shameful to reshape resource requirements for the organisation. And I have seen people met at the office door, then ushered by security to remove their effects from their office in a box and humiliatingly escorted out of the building like a convicted criminal.

None of those examples are appropriate ways for leaders to behave. None of them reflect well on the leader's character but all of them are detrimental to the organisation's culture. As I had to explain to one director, "The decision may have been right. But the way it was carried out left hundreds of people watching and asking themselves if they wanted to work for a manager or a company that treats people like that."

When someone chooses or is required to leave, it does not remove their right to be treated properly. The employee still has all the expectations of the Social Contract. They still have all the rights of the Work Contract. And an organisation should observe its own values when these events occur. Having values when everything is smooth and congenial is easy; the real test of values is when the going gets tough and in times of extreme stress for individuals and the team!

Just because someone is no longer going to work at that organisation, it does not mean they lose the right to be treated civilly, with respect and with their dignity intact. Even if someone has been justifiably fired they should still have these rights observed.

In fact, employees leaving is an excellent opportunity for the organisation to learn. Many organisations recognise this and have put in place an "exit interview" for anyone who leaves – no matter what the cause. This is usually conducted by someone impartial and respected by the individual and it gives an opportunity to explore the reasons behind the decision or their conduct. A skilful and trusted questioner will explore motivations and draw out the details of any dissatisfaction, poor leadership, or frustrations between people and from processes. Even when someone has been fired for theft there will be reasons why they took the opportunity and did not heed the consequences. There may be processes to be improved or temptations to be safeguarded against. All of this can be used to improve the culture going forward and prevent similar events from occurring again.

15 Create a tangible cultural identity

Human beings are essentially social at heart. We have an overwhelming psychological need to feel we belong to and are accepted by a group. We have a drive to be part of something bigger than ourselves that unites us with others in a common purpose. It helps us to identify with others and express who we are. It could be family, or a group of like-minded friends, a religion, work colleagues, neighbours or something else, but there is a need to feel we belong, and to give and receive attention from others.

The American psychologist Abraham Maslow first proposed his theory of motivation back in 1943. This is frequently expressed as a hierarchical pyramid of basic physical and psychological needs that humans require in order to grow, learn and develop. At the bottom of the pyramid are basic physical requirements to live: food, water, warmth, shelter to rest. Once these are satisfied, Maslow argued that humans can progress to the next stage of personal development. He stated that people require safety and security next to fulfil all their basic needs of survival before progressing further to fulfil psychological needs of feeling a sense of belonging and achieving a sense of accomplishment. It is only when all of these needs are met that individuals can go on to express their curiosity to develop and grow to their full potential.

MASLOW'S HIERARCHY OF NEEDS

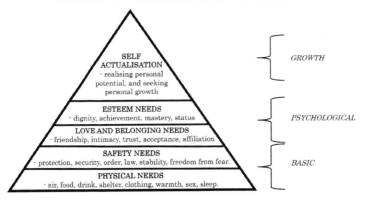

Sadly, those organisations that have poor culture health-states (e.g. chaotic and toxic) are failing to even meet the basic needs required for individuals to perform in their organisation. If people are afraid for their job or intimidated by Casual Leaders they cannot be co-operative and part of an efficient team. Individuals are too concerned with protecting themselves from threats *within* the organisation to be proactive in pursuing and progressing the interests of the organisation in the *outside* world.

Moreover, an organisation cannot truly progress to an engaged culture unless it forges a cultural identity for itself with which people can identify and which they can affiliate themselves to. Unless the organisation creates a sense of being something different, under which people can unify as an identity and an experience, the culture will only ever be a marriage of convenience in delivering its purpose. Something that will do until something better comes along.

Since Maslow's first publication, there has been an emerging theory in psychology that has built on and explored his hypothesis – sociocultural theory. There have been a number of studies that have validated and developed his thinking, and also shown the power of role models on organisational cultures. It seems clear that the need to belong and form attachments is a universal drive amongst people. We all need a certain number of regular, satisfying social interactions and this leads us to create social bonds easily. If we feel included we feel happiness, calm, satisfaction, commitment; it validates us, improves our self-esteem and leads to greater conformity and co-operation with the group. It becomes a positive reinforcement and studies of schools and colleges show it leads to higher achievement and lower dropout rates too.

The armed services and the All Blacks have shown how important a sense of cultural identity can be in forging a high-performance environment. So why do so many organisations ignore this opportunity?

Of course, not all do. In his autobiography *Made in America*, Sam Walton reveals that he wanted to seize every good idea he came across in his bid to make Walmart one of the biggest retailers in the world. One of those ideas he copied from a tennis ball supplier near Seoul and has become the famous "Walmart Cheer". Thousands of Walmart employees every day start their shifts, training activities or meetings with a chant: "Give me a W-A-L-M-A-R-T", with the rest of the people in the room shouting back the same letter; then, "What's that spell? Walmart! What's that spell? Walmart! Who's number one? THE CUSTOMER!"

It may feel a bit cringeworthy. And it must be easy for the cynics or self-conscious to deride it. But I think the Walmart Cheer is an essential part of their culture, unifying all employees in a unique experience together and enforcing awareness of their purpose in putting the customer first. In many ways the Walmart Cheer is their version of the All Blacks' Haka.

For employees to feel a sense of belonging and to give their emotional commitment, an organisation must first have a tangible identity to which people can affiliate and feel a bond with. But that identity has to have substance. It must be tangible and different. It must be something that people can identify with, feel proud of and want to be associated with. Vagueness will not suffice and pure economic drivers will not create a sense of affiliation.

Every organisation has a history. Every organisation has a purpose. Every organisation has a way in which they contribute to the good of the wider society and environment in which they operate. And every organisation has heroes who have gone beyond the call of duty in delivering the success of that organisation today. All of these can be pulled together to create a unique and unifying cultural identity for all employees to be proud of and want to contribute towards. If the organisation can also build its own traditions and customs, this helps to build a sense of permanence and continuity: a society worth belonging to.

For example, I know a media agency in London has hung a ship's bell on the main stairwell of their open-plan office. It does not matter which floor you are on; you will hear that bell toll. And every member of staff is encouraged to ring the bell to announce a significant new event worth celebrating, e.g. a new client or the first airing of a new TV commercial. Another example I know of is an organisation that celebrates its retail staff by displaying photos within their head office of anyone who receives customer praise for service. It's a fantastic bridge between store staff and their support colleagues while underlining the purpose of the company in delivering the best of customer service.

In addition, I would encourage all organisations to try to achieve independent recognition and endorsement – and then publicise such an award. A five-star Trustpilot review; a five-star Food Hygiene Award; an Outstanding from Ofsted; a Michelin star; a recommendation from customers; a Best Toilet award. It doesn't matter what it is; it matters what it represents – superior performance and approval of the efforts of your organisation and the individuals in it working as a team. And the more awards, the better. It all goes to help build a sense of identity and achievement for the whole organisation. External awards are an independent endorsement. They bring a sense of pride to the organisation through recognition and will help in recruiting the right people in the future. They should be exhibited internally for all to see – not in reception just for visitors or in the boardroom but in a major communal area with high employee footfall for greatest visibility.

All of these things take time, effort and commitment by an organisation but the benefits will make it more than worthwhile.

16 Induct people thoroughly into your culture

First impressions count. How much effort do most organisations put into creating a welcome for new staff? If a cultural identity is important for creating affiliation and belonging, how important is the introduction to create a sense of belonging and acceptance?

I have been totally underwhelmed by my own inductions in the past, twice just being shown a desk and left to get on with it, and once a full day of admin checks to ensure that my CV was not based on lies. But the experience of one friend was breathtaking in its casual approach. When he presented himself on the first day at reception he was left there all day. It soon became apparent that they had forgotten his appointment and were not prepared for him at all. Eventually he was sent off on placement for three months as a trainee salesman before he could start his marketing career.

It is not difficult to give a good impression and start the relationship on the right foot. But it does require some interest and thought. For me, a good induction would include the following:

o   Prompt greeting on arrival at reception by the immediate line manager.
o   Orientation of the building and permanent fixtures, e.g. desk, canteen, toilets etc.
o   Introduction to rest of the team and an appointed "buddy" at the same rank who will help them through the detail of performing tasks, accompany them initially on coffee breaks and to meals until the new employee creates their own circle of friends.
o   All equipment to be available with appropriate training. To include passwords, business cards etc. so that the newbie can be fully functioning ASAP.

o Introduction and training on all software and standard reports.

o Handing over the Employee Handbook and talking through the purpose, values and cultural identity of the organisation.

o Confirming the individual's staff number, their benefits, the expenses process and banking details for salary payment.

o Relevant but concise briefing documents available for absorption over the next few weeks when time allows.

o Handing over a personalised calendar pre-populated with the meeting schedules and key contact appointments so that the new joiner gets a feel for the organisation's rhythm and meets the most relevant internal and external contacts ASAP.

o A social lunch arranged for their first week so the new employee can meet more colleagues informally.

o Arranging a director's feedback meeting after three weeks to capture any points of concern and ensure the new joiner is starting to settle in.

o Giving a probationary review after three months so that formal feedback can be given by the line manager including a 360-degree assessment by other colleagues.

17 Put people-development and talent management onto the agenda

Organisations must make their leaders responsible for the people who report to them.

Everything else is measured. Everything else has an owner who is held responsible. There is no budget that is not measured, no expense that is not reported on. But often people are not included in these reports and reviews. How can an organisation expect the benefits of an "engaged" culture if it does not know what it looks like, does not put any effort into achieving it and does not put in effective measurement for progress?

Organisations have to wake up to this fact. The loss of performance from poor leadership is huge. The waste of talent and potential is criminal. The best way to deliver a sustained performance into the future must be from harnessing all the talent available and creating a vibrant, trusting and effective team-working environment.

There is no real excuse. I have suggested some simple but highly practical ways to put in effective measurement. I am sure much more talented people than me could suggest more imaginative and effective methodology. But to do nothing is ridiculous.

A good starting point is an annual plan that includes how the organisation is to maximise the potential of their people. It could be better systems and processes for more accurate and faster decision-making. It could be identifying skills and experiences worth investing in through training. It could be development of a cadre of senior managers as part of the succession plan. At the minimum it should be setting out the culture desired, the rationale and methodology to create it and the measurement of progress towards that goal.

Every year there will be a strategy brainstorm for the board to shape the annual plan and also to take a view on the development of the organisation in the next few years. Why is the same level of effort and planning not put into managing the talent that is within the organisation already? Identify the senior cadre of leaders; discuss their development needs; ensure movement of key people across the organisation to expand their skill set; and cross-pollinate best practice in leadership.

In addition, each monthly board agenda should be more than treating people as just numbers or a resource to report in terms of cost, sickness, absenteeism etc. Measure training, motivation, engagement etc. Discuss training plans and development opportunities.

Include people in every one-to-one with each people-manager. Identify weaknesses and strengths of individuals and teams. Put in effective plans for training, coaching, mentoring so that progress can be made – and ensure it happens!

Remind people-managers of their responsibilities through their job descriptions and appraisals. They have to be role models; they have to live the values and they have to develop their people. Put in effective rewards in terms of bonus payments for achievement of stretching targets; and put in consequences for poor behaviour or poor performance.

18 Ensure all work-streams and performance measures have S.M.A.R.T. objectives

It is amazing how often a work-stream disappears because no one is being held responsible for delivering it and reporting back on it. Or the work-stream is completed and no one knows if the result is impressive or poor because no objective was set for the expected performance. Or, worse still, it's the bonus objective and has been written so subjectively that payment could be, or may not be, paid because it is just an opinion if it has been achieved.

All this subjectivity and inefficiency can be avoided with a little time up front asking the questions: "What do we think will happen and what does 'good' look like?" And then writing it down in a structured and disciplined way. After all, if something is worth doing, worth giving resource in time, effort and money, then surely it is worth writing down?

Various people have been given credit for proposing the S.M.A.R.T. objective-setting acronym. It is claimed it can be traced back in various forms to Paul J. Meyer in the 1970s but was also the title of a paper published in 1981 by George T. Doran: "There's a S.M.A.R.T. way to write Managements

Goals and Objectives". Doran did not claim to be the sole author but a facilitator for the consultancy he worked for and was most probably influenced by his previous career as a director of corporate planning. He did not believe that good objectives had to include all five of the criteria every time but proposed that it was a great way to ensure that everything had been considered to achieve a goal.

Doran's paper set out the acronym for setting objectives as follows:

S – Specific (What is the area for improvement?)
M – Measurable (How will progress be expressed?)
A – Assignable (Who will do it?)
R – Realistic (What can be achieved with available resources?)
T – Time-related (When will it be achieved?)

NB There are several variations of this methodology. This seems to be because people respect the approach and have tried to apply it to a wide variety of work-streams: the annual plan, personal appraisals, projects, investments etc. I have found myself doing the same over the years and have suggested some detailed criteria to consider, below.

S.M.A.R.T. OBJECTIVES

S	What is SPECIFICALLY proposed? Does it fit with STRATEGY? Does it make SENSE? What does SUCCESS look like?
M	Who is it MOTIVATING; why and how? How will it be MEASURED and at what MILESTONES?
A	Is there an ARCI? Has the ACCOUNTABLE person AGREED the objectives? Are the objectives AMBITIOUS and ACHIEVABLE? Have ALTERNATIVE plans been considered? Why is this preferred? Are there clear ACTIONS for the way to progress? How will it give the organisation ADVANTAGE with customers against competitors?
R	Have assumptions been RESEARCHED and verified? Have RESOURCES been identified and allocated? Are resources REALISTIC for Trial? Are they realistic for full implementation? What REWARDS are required to incentivise execution? Has RETURN ON INVESTMENT been calculated? Have desired RESULTS been identified, quantified and are they REASONABLE? Has the RESPONSIBLE person accepted and committed to this plan?
T	Have assumptions been TESTED? Have TIMINGS been set against milestones? Is TRACKING in place? Is it TIME-BOUND for completion?

Whichever way an organisation wants to frame the S.M.A.R.T. objective matrix, it is a useful self-discipline to maximise time, effort and resource to be effective.

SELF-AWARENESS AND EFFECTIVE CRITICISM

Self-awareness and the ability to give others effective, positive criticism and constructive feedback have been constant themes in this book. They seem to me to be critical skills to create a positive and engaged culture and to develop competent, confident individuals who will work effectively and collaboratively in team situations. These are essential skills and competencies for good leaders, in my view. And, yet, organisations do not seem to recognise this or fail to ensure that these competencies are developed and displayed by their leaders.

The All Blacks have a saying that feedback should be "A punch to the belly, not a stab in the back". But I have found that many people within organisations lack the courage and conviction to face a potential confrontation. It requires two people, of course, to have the right attitude and for both to give and accept feedback in the right spirit. It need not be hard. Simple processes and an easily learned set of skills ensures that this could be best practice throughout organisations, enabling and engaging employees in a proactive and positive way.

An effective and objective appraisal system gives consistent opportunities up the line of management to develop these skills in a formal process. However, they do not give the opportunity to give feedback to colleagues at the same level or not within your own chain of reporting. In these cases informal processes may need to be put in place.

One informal process I have found exceptionally powerful in generating self-awareness in a practical way is the personal improvement grid – aka the PIG grid for short.

I take no credit for this idea, which was introduced to me over twenty-five years ago by a new recruit who had seen it in action in their previous company. I have used it ever since and it has proved itself to be an invaluable tool in creating relationships in a safe and pragmatic way. Frequently, I have invited my direct reports to complete this process with myself and amongst themselves; it has often been approached with wariness but always been endorsed following first trial. It is so useful that four companies I have worked for have subsequently adapted it into their appraisal processes as seen in the previous section.

Like so many good ideas, it is highly simple. It takes the form of a one-page proforma which you invite someone to complete on you while you complete it on them. You then swap the proforma and DO NOT look at it until in a safe and private location where you can reflect on the feedback you have been given. It ensures a balanced scorecard of feedback by ensuring you recognise the individual as a person, affirming their strengths, while asking them to address behaviours or start new ones which would be helpful. It is essentially democratic and puts everyone on the same playing field regardless of status, hierarchy, experience, gender or age. It is not bound by the calendar of the organisation and can be completed by two willing individuals at any time of their choice. It is confidential and respectful. At its best it is a simple form of open, honest and direct communication from one unique and talented individual to another and delivered in a safe way.

PIG GRID

I value _____ as a fellow human being because....	Please CONTINUE (as it is valuable to me in my job)....
Please STOP (as I find it unhelpful)....	Please START (as it would help me in my job)....

With goodwill _____ (signed)

The PIG grid is not a magic remedy. While I have found it highly effective it does not work with everyone. It requires two willing participants who are prepared to listen and take on each other's points of views. This demands goodwill, openness, honesty, humility, a healthy self-esteem and an adult mindset from each participant.

Only one colleague I have tried it with reacted poorly. I was feeding back to him that in my view he had no right to shout and swear at junior colleagues. He started off being bemused at the process and then became increasingly belligerent and aggressive in trying to defend his behaviours. The behaviour I was critiquing was that of the Critical Parent mindset but he was unable to accept it and responded as an Adapted Child. He was unable to understand that feedback on some aspects of his behaviour was not condemning him in his entirety as a whole person. He just could not do it. It was as if admitting he was not perfect at everything meant he must be imperfect in everything. This is not a sign of an adult mindset or of a healthy self-esteem. It was not a success, but you cannot win them all. Most people do react well and have gone onto adopt the process for themselves, with others, as they have confidence in the results.

There is a skill that needs to be developed both for the PIG grid and in other informal feedback conversations. Too often, feedback can be delivered in a negative and destructive way. And any leader will find that, in nearly every interaction, this skill of feedback is required in the course of each working day. Criticism that is delivered badly will have effects that are usually not intended, e.g. making people withdraw emotionally, closing down their listening and thinking and becoming defensive, rather than opening them up to consider balanced and helpful advice.

The goal in constructive criticism is to critique an individual in such a way that they will benefit or improve. The aim is to improve performance, output or work habits.

Randy Garner, in his book *Constructing Effective Criticism*, identifies the three key elements as:

1   Being problem-focussed, rather than personal.
2   Being specific, not vague.
3   Being descriptive, not judgemental or blaming.

He then recommends the use of one of three different techniques:

o   The "I guess no one explained to you", where criticism is deliberately crafted to act as if the person did not know the right way to do something through no fault of their own.
o   The "demonstration" method, as research has shown that the fastest way for someone to learn something and to improve is by having it modelled for them.
o   The "Sh*t Sandwich", where a positive start and finish to feedback holds a filling which might be quite critical. Even if you do not have something worth praising, just telling them you have faith in them and their abilities can have enormous positive benefits, as recently articled in the *Harvard Business Review*.

Garner has many useful tips beyond these techniques such as: choosing the place, to avoid an audience; choosing the time, to increase receptivity; reviewing the assumptions to ensure clarity of objectives; keeping the feedback impersonal and focussed on the output not the individual; maintaining objectivity and respectfulness, and being aware of your own emotions, tone of voice and body language. But, of course, fairness, accuracy, objectivity and honesty should be paramount.

SYNOPSIS OF SECTION THREE

The FRC guidelines on good corporate governance are clear. The CEO is accountable for the organisation's culture and the board is responsible for delivering it through their people. They have to role-model it themselves and put effective measurement in place.

It is worthwhile. Goleman and McClelland have shown that an "engaged" culture delivers a superior performance but it does take time and relentless attention to detail. Not everyone will make the grade.

James Kerr reveals that the All Blacks have a philosophy that helped build their culture: "Be a good ancestor" and "Plant trees you will never see". It is about commitment and sustainability. It is about building something substantial for the future. Sadly, there are many short-term pressures on organisations today – we want results now. This, plus the short tenure of CEOs, means that many organisations have not planted the trees for an engaged culture and the board's legacy has been to be a poor ancestor.

It is easy to make a start from which the culture can grow. All it takes is for the CEO and the board to demonstrate the required willpower. I have suggested simple structural and process changes that at least start to measure and progress the right culture. It is not forgivable for a future survey to find that board directors do not discuss culture and do not know what it should be.

However, it is also very difficult to move an existing culture to an engaged health state – particularly if the start point is as bad as a toxic culture. Directors will need to be committed; managers will have to be held responsible; employees will need to see a tangible difference; otherwise the inertia of the culture will not change. Starting the ball rolling will take a lot of effort and it will take remorseless persistence before a positive momentum will be felt. It may well be that a number of Casual Leaders will have to be cut out of the organisation if they fail to change or resist the process – and that is not an easy decision to make or execute well. But no matter how difficult it is... let's be clear... it's the CEO's and board's job! And if they do not start doing it then they are guilty of being Casual Leaders themselves.

Section four

KNOW THE VALUE OF VALUES

The weak sunshine peered through dirty windows and made the dust sparkle as it slowly drifted in the air. We could hear the traffic outside the walls and the busy actions of the cleaners in the recesses of the hotel. It was a tired and musty meeting room, typical of many three-star hotels around the country. At one time the decoration would have been considered funky and cheerful. Now it was faded and bruised by years of use. It smelt vaguely of past meals and stale sweat. The seating was arranged in a circle. It was the usual: uncomfortable armless dining chairs that stack. Designed for a one-hour meal, we would be seated on them for the next two days. A familiar enough environment for our meetings but an unfamiliar agenda – a values workshop.

It was 9am. All the directors were seated and cheerfully swapping banter with each other. They were a tight-knit team who had worked together for years; they respected each other and sales had been good recently. Life felt good and they were relaxed in each other's company. The facilitator stood up, the chatter stopped, and he introduced himself. The facilitator invited each of us to volunteer our own personal values to start the workshop. It all went deadly quiet. Everyone felt awkward suddenly. There was much shuffling of feet and colleagues looked around desperately hoping that someone else would start talking. The average age was forty years old but you would have thought we were back at school as we sat in uncomfortable silence for minutes. Self-conscious? Not wanting to share something so intimate? Unwilling to talk about personal beliefs? Struggling to understand what was meant? Not wanting to appear stupid!

Eventually someone suggested that "family" was his main value. There was a general murmur of relief and a muttering of agreement from everyone else. That felt like safe ground. That felt right and would be above criticism or looking stupid. We were all right... and we were all wrong!

WHEN IS A VALUE NOT A VALUE?

At the outset of this book, I said there was lots of confusion about values and what they are. The introductory story to this section illustrates that values are not a familiar concept and therefore they are not a comfortable discussion point for many people – even for seasoned and mature business professionals with many years' experience of people-management. For the vast majority of people, development of their values has been a subconscious process and they do not wear them on their sleeve. They have become an intuitive feeling of what is right or wrong rather than a rational and highly debated process to form their conscience.

I am sure this is partly because there are many different phrases that are bandied around: personal values, corporate values, core values, society values, family values etc. We nod our heads and have a vague understanding of what they mean but have never interrogated them in detail. They do not form a conscious part of ourselves at the forefront of our thinking. And some commentators have confused our understanding further, such as Professor Shalom Schwartz, who was really talking about our motivations or drivers behind our behaviour rather than the actual behaviour itself. Or those commentators who talk about "brand values", which are frequently about physical features or attributes, iconography or imagery, and emotional benefits or emotional associations that a brand wants to express, rather than the behaviours of the people who deliver the brand, e.g. Kerr reveals that two All Black brand values are "New Zealand" and "masculinity". There are even some commentators who have tied themselves in knots trying to explain the difference between values, ethics, principles, morals and the law. And there are even more commentators or organisations that refer to their values but are actually talking about competencies or skills. It is all very confusing!

I have experienced all the things listed above. It has never been satisfactory for me. I have not been able to rationalise and absorb more than the direction or intent of these statements. Sometimes it feels like commentators are dancing on the head of a pin trying to explain the finessed details between each concept. And that is not the point of this book. I want to give practical and simple guidance to all levels of an organisation not just the intellectual or academic circles. I am in the camp that, if you cannot explain something simply, then you haven't explained anything at all.

I believe many commentators are confusing completely different concepts. They are mixing up: ambitions, motivations, beliefs, behaviour, ability and talent. There are blurred lines between what is formative of our character, the manifestations of our character, and what is either a natural ability or a learned skill.

There are of course things that we value (i.e. think valuable or worth something) that are not a value in themselves. For example, we may value our family, but family is not a behaviour and therefore it is not a value. What do we mean by family anyway? Do we mean family financial security? Family harmony? Family happiness? Family safety? Or that the members of our family are our number one priority and therefore we feel responsibility for them? Or is it that family is a source of our own emotional security? Or is it a combination of all of these? Either way, the concept of family will drive a number of our behaviours to achieve what we desire but family is not a behaviour in itself. In fact family is a motivation which is implicit from a combination of some of Schwartz's list of ten motivations: benevolence, conformity, security, tradition and universalism. So all the directors in that story were wrong!

Something we value is not a value if it is really a motivation. There are many things which we aspire to, which we are ambitious to achieve, that will drive our intent and our subsequent behaviours *but* are not values. And family is one of them.

So I have created my own list of what I believe are the core motivations of people but are not values. These are concepts that we think worthwhile, that we value but are not values in themselves. They are the concepts that are formative of our character but are not the expression or manifestations of our character. They are our ambitions, our motivations, the cause of our intent and the drivers of some of our behaviours – but are not social behaviours in themselves. I have adopted Schwartz's methodology and included others that are implicit or more current language in our conversations today. I believe these give us a purpose in life. They are our core drivers and the things that motivate us most. They are the things that make us get out of bed and get out there into the big wide world. They are formative of our character but are not our character itself because that comes from the strength of our social beliefs and the convictions that drive our behaviour and attitudes to others.

FORMATIVE OF CHARACTER
AMBITIONS, MOTIVATIONS, DRIVERS AND INTENT

THINGS WE VALUE THAT ARE CONCEPTUAL

A World at Peace	Happiness	Quality
Achievement	Harmony	Safety
Adventure	Health	Self-Direction
Ambition	Hedonism	Self-Esteem
Appreciation of Beauty	Hope	Self-Respect
Benevolence	Imagination	Sensuality
Challenge	Independence	Simplicity
Comfort	Inner Harmony	Social Recognition
Confidence	Intuition	Spirituality
Conformity	Job Security	Stability
Control	Justice	Status
Dominance	Love	Stimulation
Environment	Making a Difference	Success
Excellence	National Security	Tradition
Excitement	Novelty	Trust
Experiences	Personal Fulfilment	Universalism
Exploring	Personal Growth	Vision
Family	Pleasure	Wealth
Financial Stability	Power	Wisdom
Freedom	Prestige	
Friendships	Pride	
Future Generations		

And then there are other things that we value or organisations desire which are also not values but competencies.

For example, I worked for one company that listed amongst its values execution, customer focus and results. You might think at first sight that these are values and essential behaviours to deliver the company's purpose. However, I believe that they are distinctly competencies – something that is derived from our natural ability or a skill that we have learned. They may be desirable for an organisation but they are not manifestations of our social rules and our beliefs about the right attitudes and behaviours towards others. So you can learn the skills that are necessary for leadership, but that does not make you a leader because that comes from your strength of character or values.

On the next page are illustrations of the other competencies that an organisation might want to have in order to achieve their mission or purpose:

COMPETENCIES

NATURAL ABILITY AND LEARNED SKILLS

COMPETENCIES DESIRED BY ORGANISATIONS

Adaptability	Follow-Through	Personal Drive/Energy
Analysis	Influencing Skills	Personal Impact
Assertiveness	Initiative	Perspective
Attention to detail	Innovation	Persuasiveness
Building Capability	Inspiring	Planning
Challenging Others	Intellect	Problem-Solving
Clarity of Communication	Interpreting People	Quality of Work
Competence	Judgement	Quality Results
Competitiveness	Leadership	Reasoning
Compliance	Logic	Responsive to Challenge
Conflict Resolution	Managing Budgets	Results Orientation
Context Sensitivity	Managing People	Risk-Taking
Conviction	Mental Agility	Self-Development
Creativity	Mission Focus	Service-Orientated
Curiosity	Motivating	Skills
Customer Focus	Multi-Tasking	Strategic Thinking
Decisiveness	Negotiating	Task Focus
Demanding	Numeracy	Teamwork
Efficiency	Obedience	Technical Skills
Effort	Organised	Understanding Organisations
Endurance		Winning Mentality
Energy		Work Ethic
Entrepreneurial		Work Rate
Execution		

While motivations and competencies are valuable and worthwhile in their own right, they are not values in themselves. And many organisations have managed to confuse us by not being precise in what they have stated as their values – the standards of behaviours they want. If people do not understand exactly what you are talking about then you are setting yourself up to fail. Confusion and miscommunication at the outset will hardly help with delivery and action in following through the intent. If you want to cut down a tree, first sharpen your axe.

At the outset I defined values as the basic rules of how to live in reasonable harmony with other people. This is the base state and common to all of us as we will have formed them from a very early age of our development. We all have them – our own personal values. We all have our own personal, unwritten rules on the right way to behave and the right attitude to have towards others. Subconsciously we have all worked out what are the appropriate social behaviours that encourage harmony and co-operation. They form a critical part of our attitude to life and to other people; they are the result of our beliefs and the drivers of our actions. Our personal values are the key principles we have been taught or have observed, or have experienced, and adopted for ourselves as a kind of social etiquette. Our personal values help us to make decisions on what is right or wrong, what we should or shouldn't do, what is good or bad. And this basic set of universal rules form our Social Contract with each other in any context.

As we get older this definition of values can become more developed for some people. For those people that have developed an understanding of the wider social context – those that have developed their self-awareness, emotional intelligence and social intelligence – the definition of values becomes more sophisticated. Now these rules of behaviour can not just become the way to live in reasonable harmony with others but can also be the best version of ourselves in improving the community or society in which we live.

Whereas our motivational drivers are essentially self-interested and come from our need to survive and personally thrive, our values are primarily there to overcome our selfish needs and are the glue to building healthy relationship built on mutual interests and co-operation. Our motivational drivers are the concepts and desires that form our character but our values are the expression of our character. When people are described as having strength of character we are acknowledging their commitment to a number of social beliefs and their resolution to behave in the right, unselfish way for the benefit of society. The stronger their belief, the greater their conviction. And some people are so committed to their beliefs that they become truly principled people and their values are an indelible expression of their character. As Massey argued, these people are truly few and far between; think of Gandhi, Martin Luther King and Nelson Mandela.

The distinction that I am trying to make is that:

o **Motivations are what you want**
o **Competencies are what you can do**
o **But values are who you are**

Your motivations can be taken from you. You can lose heart, lose focus. You can lose wealth, status, your health, get divorced or even be ostracised from your social group. You can be a victim of war, terrorism or criminality. You can suffer financial stress or be isolated from others, through no fault of your own.

Similarly your competencies can be eroded. You may lose natural abilities such as mental capacity or athleticism. You may find that old skills are no longer required and you have to retrain to be competent again. You may find that there is no outlet or demand for your ability or skill. Your ability to learn may become impaired.

Neither motivations nor competencies are the source of personal self-esteem although they can give you that illusion. The true source of self-esteem comes from your values. They are not something you desire nor are they something you can learn or can "do" by a fortunate accident of biology and inherited genes. Values are what make you worth something as a person. While everything else can be taken away, no one can take away your belief in the right way to behave as a valuable and positive contributor to your social group. It is your values that distinguish your character and it is values that make you worthwhile. They are the ultimate expression of your essence – your humanity.

OUR CHARACTER

SOCIAL BELIEFS MANIFESTED IN OUR ATTITUDES & BEHAVIOURS TO OTHERS

VALUES OR PERSONAL BEHAVIOURS

Acceptance of Others	Fairness	Passion
Accountability	Faithful	Patience
Appreciation	Forgiveness	Perseverance
Authenticity	Friendliness	Politeness
Balance (Home/Work)	Fun	Positivity
Broad Minded	Generosity	Privacy
Caring	Gentleness	Protecting the Vulnerable
Cheerfulness	Goodwill	Prudence
Civility	Gratitude	Pulling Your Weight
Cleanliness	Hard work	Quality of Interaction
Commitment	Healthy Living	Reasonableness
Community Involvement	Helpfulness	Receptiveness to Experiences
Compassion	Honesty	Recognition of Others
Compromise	Honour	Reliability
Conscientiousness	Humility	Respect
Consideration	Humour	Responsibility
Consistency	Inclusive	Responsiveness

Co-operation with Others	Integrity	Risk-Taking
Courage	Interest in Others	Self-Discipline
Courtesy	Keeping Confidences	Self-Improvement
Creativity	Keeping Promises	Selflessness
Dependability	Kindness	Self-Sacrifice
Dignity	Learning	Sensitivity
Diligence	Listening	Sharing
Diplomacy	Loyalty	Sincerity
Diversity	Meeting Obligations	Support
Doing Your Fair Share	Mercy	Sympathy
Ease with Uncertainty	Non-judgemental	Tact
Empathy	Non-violent	Timeliness
Encouragement	Open-Minded	Tolerance
Enthusiasm	Openness	Trusting
Equality	Optimism	Trustworthiness
Exceeding Expectations		Unthreatening
Exclusivity		Vitality

TRUST IS THE KEY

Trust is the glue of life. It's the most essential ingredient in effective communication. It's the foundation principle that holds all relationships.

– Stephen Covey

So what is the value of values to an organisation? They are a written code of standards selecting the most appropriate behaviours from our own unwritten personal values to deliver a common and focussed society or culture. They are cohesive, communal, social behaviours that build harmony. They are actionable and purposeful and they are standards that an organisation declares it will hold itself to. Ultimately they are there to counter our own selfish instincts and a control to prevent us putting ourselves ahead of other people. They create a sense of belonging to a common cause and group. They guide us in decision-making and help to predict another person's behaviour. They give us a shared purpose and a framework from which we can prioritise and evaluate alternatives. Fundamentally, they are there to establish trust between individuals, build co-operation, enable communication and forge efficient teamwork. It is all about building an engaged and healthy culture.

Trust is a firm belief in the reliability, truth or ability of someone. It is a conviction. It is an absolute. You either trust someone or you do not. There is no halfway house. You cannot trust someone with your feelings but not with your reputation. You cannot trust someone for their competency but not for their honesty. You cannot trust someone for their intent but not their reliability. You do not trust people with your money but not with your confidences. Trust is all-enveloping – you either give it or you do not. It is a personal commitment and is not given lightly. It makes us vulnerable and brings our emotions into play with our interactions with others. The loss of trust is as painful as a physical injury since we have given something of our being which has been injured and it brings a huge sense of rejection. When our trust is broken we go through all the phases and symptoms of a grieving process: disbelief, anger, bargaining and depression. And yet, as we know well, if we get to a position of mutual trust it is a wonderful feeling that generates huge commitment and fulfilment. Trust is the most highly prized of all human emotions.

Blanchard's ABCD model determines trust comes from four major factors: competence, caring, integrity and reliability. It is a model I have used widely with many teams as an excellent basis for understanding what an "engaged" culture should look like. But I am not sure it goes far enough in explaining the primary role of values in delivering trust or effective teamwork.

There are at least four primary values that must be present or trust will never happen. Without these values, trust will always be impaired and remain a pipedream. And they are nothing to do with competencies: they are not an innate ability or a skill that can be learned. Either you believe in these values and behave accordingly or you do not.

The first value essential to build trust is goodwill. Goodwill is literally wishing someone well, rather than wishing them ill. But it is also accepting people at face value for who they present themselves to be. It is the absence of any preconceived prejudices or negative expectations. It is about being reasonable and non-judgemental. It is an attitude of friendliness and co-operation based on no prior evidence. It is being open-minded and being willing to behave and relate to another in good faith.

You might think that this should not need to be stated but I can assure you that the reality of organisations can be very different. I can remember joining one organisation and the prevailing attitude was: "So you think you are good enough to join us? Who are you anyway? Where have you come from? We are the best and we will make up our own mind about you. The jury is out for three months so we can judge if you are good enough to be one of us. We will not be helpful or friendly until then." Contrast this attitude with that of another organisation I joined: "So you are the new manager? You must be the best in the world at what you do if we picked you. We are so lucky to have you. Welcome! It's great to meet you. How can I help you? What do you need?" Goodwill was the difference. Sometimes I have been accused of naivety but I would prefer to offer someone goodwill until they prove they don't deserve it rather than greet them with suspicion and cynicism. I know which organisation I preferred to work in.

Another essential value to deliver trust is respect. Respect has to be mutual. No one gives respect if they are given disrespect in return. Respect does not need to go as far as admiration but it is essentially regard for someone else's feelings, rights, wishes or abilities. It is recognition that everyone else has just as much right to breathe and think as ourselves. They may have different priorities, competencies, abilities or even status but it does not make them any less important that ourselves. It is a fundamental value that contributes to politeness, courtesy and civility. Respect underpins the Social Contract and without it the prospect of establishing trust is lost.

Honesty is essential. Both your own and theirs. Without this value how can trust be built? If you do not believe what someone has said, on what basis can trust be built? You will always be checking facts or sources of information; your head will be filled with doubt. People will make mistakes; they will say things that they believe to be true but later turn out that they were misinformed. It is the intent and the ownership that really matters; this is when honesty is really tested. If someone accepts they were wrong and does not cover it up, hide the truth or just hopes no one finds out – that is the real test of honesty. Your word is your bond within the limits of the knowledge that you held at the time.

And finally, Consistency. The absence of this behaviour is the fourth value that will prevent trust being formed. Given the choice, employees would prefer leaders or colleagues that were consistent in their behaviour, even if they did not agree with it or thought it poor, rather than volatility and unpredictability. If someone is consistent, you know where they are coming from and can anticipate behaviours or reactions. Consistency brings reliability, dependability and certainty. We know where we stand and for right or for wrong we can expect a certain behaviour or reaction to similar events. Even if that means your leader is consistently hypocritical or abuses the Social Contract at least we know that is what will happen. However, unpredictability or subjective behaviours give us no certainty and just leave us stressed not knowing what to expect. Without consistency there is no basis for any relationship let alone building one of trust.

And there is one other value that is vital and that will do more than any other to develop trust. In my view it is the most important behaviour of them all – but I will set out the case for it in the next chapter.

Trust is essential between individuals but it is important, also, when we work together within a group, which we call teamwork. I have listed teamwork as a competency as it can be a learned skill but it totally relies on each individual to share certain values if it is to be the most effective team. For example, you may not trust an individual but you might respect their competency or their experience. This would not necessarily prevent a team from delivering on a task but it would make it less effective and enjoyable. But there are other values or behaviours that are also called for to create an effective team.

For example, can you have effective teamwork if you do not share a broad acceptance of others? Or accept responsibility? Or appreciate each individual? Some of the other essential values to create an effective team would include: civility, commitment, compromise, consideration, co-operation, dependability, diligence, doing your fair share, empathy, helpfulness, keeping promises, listening, meeting obligations, open-mindedness, reasonableness, recognition, sharing and support.

Shared values are essential if an engaged culture is to emerge in an organisation. Unless these are present, and adhered to, the prospect of positive relationships, effective transactions between individuals and engaged teams are all frustrated. And it starts at the top. The CEO and the board have to be trustworthy – literally worthy of trust – in the eyes of their management and employees for trust to infuse the culture.

The desired values cannot occur naturally in an organisation if they are not an indelible part of the way you go about doing your business. They are beliefs that are evidenced through the behaviour and attitudes of everyone. They have to be role-modelled and be an essential part of everyone's character. Even then, as Massey pointed out, we will follow those rules only so long as we think we need to. We will still break these values occasionally, especially if we feel threatened, or if we are in a stressful situation, or we think that no one will see us doing it. So it is of primary importance that the values become embedded in every facet of the day-to-day function of the organisation and that the appropriate behaviours have high visibility and approval. Conversely, inappropriate behaviours have to be called out for what they are and attract consequences or organisations will find themselves in all sorts of trouble.

Values build trust outside the organisation too. They are essential for good practice and in attracting customers. There have been many recent examples where the stated values of an organisation has not been a reality in the way they behave.

Wells Fargo is the fourth largest bank in America and one of the biggest businesses worldwide. In its 2015 annual report the chairman and chief executive officer, John G. Stumpf, is quoted widely: "We never take for granted the trust our customers have placed in us... We put our customers first and treat them as our valued guests... We are committed to our customers' satisfaction and financial success and to work in their best interest. In short, we are on our customers' side... We want all our team members to lead by bringing our vision and values to life."

However, *Fortune* magazine reports that Wells Fargo created 2.1 million fake accounts in 2016 without customers' permission, admitted it had charged as many as 575,000 consumers for car insurance they did not need, and then revealed in 2017 that it had uncovered a further 1.4 million fake accounts that it had not previously declared. Just for the car insurance scandal, Wells Fargo is said to have paid out $80 million in remediation and cut seventy senior managers in the bank's retail banking division.

The Volkswagen 2013 annual report included a statement on the Group's code of conduct and guidelines: "which is applicable throughout the Group, provides guidance for our employees in the event of legal and ethical challenges in their daily work. It embodies the Group values of closeness to customers, maximum performance, creating value, renewability, respect, responsibility and sustainability. All employees are equally responsible for adhering to these."

The Volkswagen CO_2 scandal erupted in September 2015, when the company admitted that nearly 600,000 cars sold in the US were fitted with "defeat devices", designed to circumvent emissions tests. The then head of its US operations, Michael Horn, had previously claimed at a congressional committee that the deception was the work of "a couple of software engineers". This was far from the truth that emerged when Volkswagen agreed a "statement of facts" as part of a settlement with the US Department of Justice. One indictment had even claimed that former CEO Martin Winterkorn was not only fully briefed about what his engineers were up to; he also authorised a continuing cover-up. The BBC reported it as "an 'appalling' fraud that went to the very top of the company".

Most commentators agree that values on their own are meaningless unless they are fully embraced by the organisation and evident in everyday behaviour. Many quote Enron as an example of this. Enron was a huge US energy company; it was the largest natural gas merchant in North America and the largest marketer of electricity in the United States before its collapse. In 2001 it became one of the largest bankruptcy cases ever. For years Enron had used complex business models and unethical practices to exaggerate earnings and inflate its share price. Its eventual collapse effectively destroyed one of the major accountancy firms that audited its accounts. And yet Enron's board of directors and audit committee looked like a model of corporate governance, cited as such by an influential magazine in 2000, and its core values were: communication, respect, integrity and excellence.

In each of these examples the behaviour of employees and management of these companies fell well short of the standards that one would rightfully expect. The respective boards of directors found that the behaviours that they aspired to in their public pronouncements, and many might have presumed as common decency, were not exhibited. Their organisations had abused the interests, and the Social Contracts, of their customers in spectacular ways which attracted negative headlines around the world. And some of the behaviours now look to have been illegal and even known at the most senior levels of the organisation.

In short, the directors of these businesses had worked on a presumption that the right behaviours would be shown throughout their organisation and have since had to tighten up their values. It is a case of shutting the stable door after the horse has bolted – or when they have destroyed the trust of the general public and potential customers. When it comes to the values of your organisation it is never safe to work from a presumption. If something should not need to be said, say it anyway... and then make it true.

SO WHAT VALUES SHOULD AN ORGANISATION HAVE AND HOW MANY?

It does not matter if you call them competencies or values. Just be clear on your standards, make them mean something in reality and don't confuse people. For example, one commentator has even tried to make a distinction between core values, aspirational values, permission-to-play values and accidental values.

What matters is that every organisation does need to state the natural abilities or trained skills (i.e. competencies) it needs to meet its purpose PLUS the core behaviours it needs to become an effective, positive team – an "engaged" culture. Without these the mission will be precarious and may end in failure.

In his paper "Make Your Values Mean Something", published in 2002 in the *Harvard Business Review*, Patrick Lencioni says, "Most value statements are bland, toothless or just plain dishonest. And, far from being harmless, as some executives assume, they're often highly destructive. Empty values statements create cynical and dispirited employees, alienate customers, and undermine managerial credibility."

There is no right answer to what specific values an organisation should have; that has to be determined by each organisation for themselves. But, whatever the values are, they must be meaningful and sincere, and actively role-modelled throughout an organisation – from top to bottom.

Some commentators do think there are some values that should NOT be included though. Denise Lee Yohn published her paper "Ban These 5 Words from Your Corporate Values Statement" in the *Harvard Business Review* in 2018. The values she would ban are: ethical (or integrity), teamwork (or collaboration), authentic, fun and customer-orientated (or customer-centric). She argues that these are "table stakes", or just common hygiene factors that should be expected of any business to be competitive. Her argument is that an organisation's core values should embody the differentiation of the organisation – the unique things that make the business stand out.

On "ethical" (or "integrity") Yohn says, "Every company should operate ethically and with integrity – and by stating this competency as one of your core values, you raise the question of why you have to point it out." On "teamwork", she states, "You shouldn't need to tell your people to work together – it's common sense."

I could not disagree more. Sadly, the examples that litter this book, and the scandals of recent years, show that Yohn's comments are a million miles from the reality of what is happening out there. Her critique has academic appeal but is just not the experience of people in the real world. And many of the world's largest brands don't agree either. 6Q, the Australian employee survey consultancy, published a blog on "190 Brilliant Examples of Company Values". This reveals that Accenture, Adidas, American Express, Barnes & Noble, Build-A-Bear,

Coca-Cola, Genentech, Google, Kellogg's, Nike, Proctor & Gamble, and Southwest Airlines all specifically reference integrity or customer service OR BOTH in their core values. In fact various sources estimate that between 55 and 90% of corporations incorporate values around ethics or integrity. It is so prevalent and yet the scandals keep coming, the Casual Leaders persist and many cultures are far removed from being engaged. The reality is that, if an organisation actually delivered behaviours of integrity throughout its workforce, it would be genuinely differentiated and unique!

Nor is there an answer to how many values an organisation should have. You might think a shortlist has greater opportunity to be embraced and become a vital part of the way an organisation conducts its business. However the most "toxic" culture I have come across had only three values, while the most "engaged" culture I have worked within had ten. The blog published by 6Q seems to suggest that on average most organisations have around seven core values. However it suggests also that Southwest Airlines in the US has twenty-two values (which might be excessive).

So let's go back to their original objective and determine if there might be some rules on what could be considered in creating a set of core values for an organisation.

The objective of values is to create a focussed society or culture that maximises trust and effective teamwork in order to be at optimal efficiency in delivering the purpose of the organisation.

Clearly the differentiating competencies of the organisation should be within their value set. Remember these are the natural abilities or learned skills that the organisation needs and if they recruit wisely, and train well, will give them an advantage over their competitors. This could include: "executional excellence", as Adidas desires; or "innovation", as Adobe looks for; or "customer service", as Barnes & Noble require; or just "teamwork", which

American Express claims. Or it might be socially responsible such as Ben & Jerry's, who "strive to minimise our negative impact on the environment". Many of these require a large set of firmly held beliefs in the right way to behave to be optimised, as previously illustrated for teamwork, but they are also a set of skills that can be taught and learned. However, they need not be expressed so blandly as if avoiding the danger of inspiring people.

Just because some of these standards of behaviour are generic, it does not mean they cannot be expressed in a personalised and motivating way to trigger emotion and commitment.

Bass, the large brewing and leisure retailing conglomerate in the UK at the end of the twentieth century, specialised in expressing competencies in an engaging way. Amongst their values was "building capability", which included personal development, teamwork, positive relationships, leadership styles and people-development. Also included was "strategic thinking and innovation", which ensured that creativity was focussed and purposeful to meet commercial needs. Similarly, Virgin Airlines create an explicit sense of team and ownership to make their values or competencies inspirational, including "We think customer" and "We are determined to deliver." Or Coca-Cola who create explanations that get to the heart of the value they want, e.g. "Accountability: if it is to be, it's up to me," and "Quality: what we do, we do well."

Any values list created should include behaviours as well as competencies. Lineberry emphasised the importance of energy and attitude to create the right learning environment and to create Players. Sanford detailed the need for both support and challenge to maximise performance. And Goleman emphasised the behaviours required of each leadership style; it is particularly important to capture the behaviours of the most effective style, which is Authoritative.

Not surprisingly, some organisations have tried to capture these behaviours within their values set. Vision Express, the

UK optical chain, lists "passion" as a core value as it should bring behaviours of energy and commitment with attitudes of enthusiasm and positivity. Starbucks try to embrace "support" with the following value: "Creating a culture of warmth and belonging, where everyone is welcome." Nike capture the need for "energy" with: "Simplify and go," plus, "Evolve immediately." Bass captured "challenge" and "energy" with: "Courage and conviction" as a core competency (actually a behaviour).

Some organisations capture other behaviours that they want in common across their entire workforce. Perhaps most inspirational of these is Ikea, which claims "Humbleness and willpower" as a core value. For me, this expresses both a highly attractive attitude, vital for true leadership, with a need for energy. They also have values such as "Togetherness and enthusiasm", which captures support and a positive attitude, and "Constant desire for renewal", which expresses energy, challenge and attitude. In fact, Ikea lists also a specific value around the leadership style that it wants within the business – "Accept and delegate responsibility."

Many organisations effectively combine competencies and these behaviours in the way they express their values. Famously, Intel talks of "Constructive confrontation", which pairs challenge with fundamental behaviours of goodwill, positivity, respect and courtesy. Bass talked of the "Drive for results" to capture the energy it needed from the organisation. Coca-Cola talks of teamwork as a fundamental combination of behaviour and competence – "Collaboration: leverage collective genius."

And finally, the most enlightened organisations would add further values for their most senior executives or directors. These are the most visible cadre of the organisation and the most likely to lead large groups of managers and employees. They have to be the role models and should be held accountable for the highest standards of competency but most importantly behaviour within the hierarchy. These are the people who lead others and are responsible for the most vulnerable but potentially most valuable resource of the organisation – the people. This is the cadre from which the culture will either thrive and become "engaged" or be diminished and be less effective. They will either establish trust within the organisation or create cynicism and disrespect. There can be no room for Casual Leaders in this group despite the evidence that they are prevalent. They have to be trustworthy to achieve an engaged culture of trust and effective teamwork. And there is one value that will do this more than any other!

IT ALL COMES DOWN TO THIS ONE VALUE

In his book *Leaders Eat Last,* Simon Sinek details five leadership lessons. His third leadership lesson is entitled "Integrity Matters" and in this section he states, "Building trust requires nothing more than telling the truth." I hate to disagree as I have such deep admiration for much of Simon's reasoning. However, I don't think he goes far enough in his critique. Trust requires good intentions, adult mindsets, competence and caring as well as honesty. Honesty is a fundamental part of integrity, and integrity is so much more than just honesty. Integrity is almost everything. It is the ultimate statement of good character!

I was first introduced to the concept of values in the mid-1990s. Since that time, I have held value sessions with every team I have been responsible for.

Some twenty-five years later, I must have conducted over fifty values sessions with groups that varied in size from five to eighty. They have been made up of graduate trainees, junior and senior managers, technical experts, heads of department and directors. They have worked for all sizes of companies – from small businesses to FTSE 100 PLCs. They have been in industries and markets as diverse as medicines, skin creams, hotels, pubs, restaurants, suppliers, agencies and retailers. The youngest participant was eighteen years old, the oldest fifty-four years old. They have been as diverse in sexual orientation, ethnicity, religion, birthplace, indigenous culture and gender orientation as you can imagine. Many had previous experience of a number of other countries, other companies or technical disciplines. It has been a huge cross-section of society and must number several hundred people. And yet they have all concluded a very similar set of values – and the number one value they want of others, and will personally sign up to, has always been the same.

The last team I led was no different. The values sessions always start with a real struggle to understand what we are talking about. Once they get their heads around competencies and behaviours there is always a lively discussion of people's personal drivers or motivations – family, friends, ambition etc. And then we agree a list of five to six behaviours or competencies we want from each other, our colleagues in the room, our teams, the rest of the business AND which we will promise to sign up to ourselves. The list always includes communication or enthusiasm or teamwork or customer focus or professionalism or fun or collaboration or energy or positivity – in fact around 80% of the final agreed values are the same as all previous teams I have worked for. But there is one value which is ever-present and always at the top of the list – integrity. Of the fifty-plus teams I have conducted a values session with, integrity has been the one thing they have all wanted.

Now, integrity is yet again one of those funny words that we have all heard, vaguely understand and nod our heads to without fully understanding it. When I was researching this book, integrity was just like values in having an infuriatingly wide definition dependent on what source you refer to.

The Oxford Dictionary defines integrity as:

1 The quality of being honest and having strong moral principles.
2 The state of being whole and undivided.
   2.1 The condition of being unified or sound in construction.
   2.2 Internal consistency or lack of corruption in electronic data.

And the *Business Dictionary* defines integrity as:

1 Strict adherence to a moral code, reflected in transparent honesty and complete harmony in what one thinks, says and does.
2 State of a system where it is performing its intended functions without being degraded or impaired by changes or disruptions in its internal or external environments.
3 Stored or transmitted data that is free from any unauthorised change.

While C.S. Lewis is often quoted to have said:

"INTEGRITY IS DOING THE RIGHT THING, EVEN WHEN NO ONE IS WATCHING"

Over the years, in discussions with my teams, we have even come up with our own definition of integrity. For us, integrity was "Being open and honest, doing the right thing by everyone, even when no one was watching or when it wasn't in our own best interests."

Why was this so important to us that we would try to form our own definition? Because integrity is fundamental to forging trust; it was frequently absent in many of our dealings with colleagues, and we needed to create some universal understanding amongst ourselves that would guide our actions, reactions and behaviours in every situation we would come up against in our day-to-day lives in business. We wanted to be trustworthy so we could demand trustworthy behaviours in return – it is the ultimate adult-to-adult decision.

So let's review the implications of this definition of integrity, and the discussions that went on within these teams before they all concluded that this was the most important value for them.

If you are truly open and honest, there can be no secret agenda. Your agenda is out in the open and exactly what you state it to be. You are being genuine and authentic. You are transparent. There are no Machiavellian behaviours; there is no game-playing and no gamesmanship. You do not do any politicking or plotting or scheming. You own your opinion and can back it up with the evidence to support it and a balanced version of all the facts – even those that might be contrary. You never invent data, never fabricate conversations or events. You keep promises always. What you see is what you get. What you commit to is what you will do. What you say is accurate and does not need to be checked. There are no cover-ups and you give credit where it is due.

If you are truly open, you are open-minded. Open to new ideas, different influences and prepared to understand other viewpoints than your own. You are receptive and respectful of others. You are willing to learn.

If you are truly "doing the right thing", your agenda is the best interests of your colleagues and the organisation. It cannot be for your own glory or selfish motivations. You are acting honourably, treating people in the right way. When you get things wrong you admit it. When your behaviour lapses, you apologise. You stand up to bullies and to any abuse of others. You never break the law or endanger anyone. You keep confidences. There is no grandstanding and there is no back-stabbing. There are no flamboyant gestures or initiatives designed to get headlines and build your profile but which wastes resource and everyone else's effort and time. You are upholding both the Social Contract and the Work Contract. You are coming from a place of goodwill and you have an open mind; you are extending respect to others and acknowledging both your accountability to the organisation and your responsibility to others. If you spot something wrong you do something about it – even if it is not your direct responsibility. If you see something that needs to be sorted out – a paper jam in the copier, a spill hazard, a faulty electrical lead etc. – you do something about it. You are scrupulously fair and incorruptible. You are self-regulating and have good self-control. You will meet all your obligations.

If you really do this "by everyone", you understand that your behaviours impact on more than just your immediate colleagues. Your behaviours are in line with the needs and expectations of all stakeholders in the organisation and are beneficial to your customers and society as a whole.

These stakeholders include even the lowest status employees and contracted staff – cleaners, clerks, cooks, porters or security staff. They include the shareholders and every customer in your distribution and supply chains. Stakeholders even include the professional analysts and auditors of the organisation who are paid to critique the organisation's performance. The list includes every supplier, agency or consultant that you engage with. All of these people deserve and should receive the best in trustworthy behaviours and should be reassured that you will "do the right thing" under any circumstances.

There is no excuse for ignoring, or treating badly, anyone employed or contracted to the organisation. There is no excuse for misleading shareholders or analysts to the true performance and intent of, or challenges facing, the organisation. There is no excuse for withholding payment of supplier invoices for 120–180 days if they have completed their obligations in full – you are threatening their livelihood just to improve your cash flow. The health of the organisation and its sustainability into the future relies on the collaboration and support of all these people and they deserve to receive the best behaviour in your interaction with them.

And, of course, "by everyone" includes your eventual consumers and the wider society as a whole. If your product, service or output negatively impacts on your consumers' well-being or makes society less cohesive and co-operative, then you are not doing worthwhile work. You are devoting a substantial part of your life to being a poor citizen and to not benefiting your fellow human beings. Who wants to live like that?

If you are "doing the right thing by everyone" when no one is watching or when it is not in your own interests, then you are: dependable, reliable, responsible, consistent, unselfish, industrious, autonomous, conscientious, dedicated and professional. You give the right time and energy due to people or a task, rather than give only what time you have available or avoid doing it at all. You are being a good citizen.

And there are further implications to this definition of integrity. If you are "Being open and honest, doing the right thing by everyone, even when no one was watching or when it wasn't in our own best interests," then you must have courage and you must be humble too.

It takes courage to always do the right thing even when it is not in your own interests. You are committing to upholding everyone's rights under the Social Contract and their Work Contracts. You are undertaking not only to take the legal course of action but the moral one too. It requires sacrifice; and, if no one was watching and no one knew, why would you volunteer for extra work or go the extra mile of effort? Why would you do something that may not be recognised and rewarded? Alternatively, why would you risk damage to your reputation or take responsibility for something that went wrong? Why would you admit a mistake or an error of judgement or a lapse in meeting an obligation? Why would you risk reprimand or being disciplined? Why? Because it is the right thing to do. It is because you have integrity and are trustworthy.

It takes humility or being humble to be open and honest, and recognise that there is a code of behaviour that is more important than your own needs. It takes humility to be open-minded and understand that others may have a valid viewpoint or superior contribution to you own. It takes humility to accept that others may be more intelligent, have better experience, or know more than you. It takes humility to do tasks that need doing and not feel they are beneath you. It takes humility to recognise that your own needs and interests are NOT more important than other people's.

Every single example of Casual Leadership in this book would not, could not, have happened if the leaders really had integrity!

To really have integrity, no matter what the circumstances, is a true adult mindset. It is the ultimate test and testimony of our true natures. It states that we really have character and a good moral compass. In short, it means that we are truly trustworthy, i.e. worthy of being trusted.

Below I have listed some real examples of integrity that I have experienced or witnessed in my career:

EXAMPLE ONE

It's bonus time. Bob, the marketing director, has submitted his bonus recommendations for his team. He is sitting with the HR director to formally sign off the individual payments. She says, "We cannot afford to give Nigel that much money." The marketing director replies, "I don't understand. This is not a discretionary payment in the rules of the scheme. The objectives were S.M.A.R.T. Nigel has worked extremely hard and exceeded the target."

The HR director replies, "It is too generous. Just tell him he failed to meet the target and don't give him access to the reports that showed he did."

The marketing director replied, incredulous at this suggestion, "In the profits we will declare, this amount of money is not even a rounding error of the hundredth decimal point. You are sitting in a room where one of the company's values – honesty – is on a huge poster behind you. You are the HR director and you really expect me to lie to a valued employee and cheat them of their reward for hard work? I will not do that!"

The bonus was paid in full.

EXAMPLE TWO

Bess, a marketing manager, has asked for a meeting with the group managing director who is three management grades above her in the organisation hierarchy. The group MD has ordered a product launch by the marketing manager that she disagrees with.

The group MD is intimating and aggressive at the best of times but is clearly frustrated at having his decision questioned. Recognising this, the marketing manager says, "I am very clear on our roles in this meeting, Mr Davison. You are the managing director and your job is to direct managers such as me. But I am the marketing manager and my job is to manage our products in this marketplace including the risk of any actions we take. At any time you can say to me, 'I see a bigger picture. I know things that are above your pay grade. This is the right thing to do commercially.' But you cannot refuse to listen to me and let me tell you the risks involved from my expert knowledge. That is what you pay me to do. If at the end of my detailing the facts you tell me to do it anyway, be assured I will do it willingly and fast, and more positively than anyone else in this business."

The managing director looks baffled at first and then relaxes. He allows the counterarguments to be presented. At the end he says, "Bess, I hear that you don't want to do this. I see a bigger picture. I know things that are above your pay grade. This is the right thing to do commercially. Just do it." They both smiled and left on good terms.

The product was dully launched effectively and efficiently six weeks later. It was the best launch in the company's history… And the product failed as predicted. But not due to a lack of effort, thought or commitment. It was just the wrong product for customers.

There were no recriminations.

EXAMPLE THREE

The company had not met its targets despite enormous effort and commitment from many people. Karl, the MD, wanted to reward a particular individual and said to him, "There is no company bonus for everyone. We didn't hit the criteria for a payout. But you worked so hard in your area I will give you a discretionary payment. I wish it could be more."

The individual replied, "But what about my manager? She worked just as hard as me. Will she get anything?" The MD replied, "No. I cannot afford it."

The individual thought for a moment and replied, "If she doesn't get half of that payment, I don't want it. I could not look her in the face knowing I get a reward and she didn't it."

The MD was taken aback – shocked by the sincerity and unselfishness. Both managers got half the payment each.

EXAMPLE FOUR

A new country strategy was being presented to the group CEO. It was so different to the previous strategy that it had been presented the week before to Vince, the regional director, who had approved it.

The group CEO did not like the strategy. It challenged all his prejudices on what he wanted to do but he did not have local knowledge and could not argue with the analysis. In frustration he turned to the regional director and said, "I don't recognise this analysis. Do you agree with it?" Sensing the group CEO's mood, the regional director said, "No. I don't agree with the strategy at all."

The local MD and marketing director were taken aback. And the latter said, "I am really surprised, Vince. We presented it to you last week and you not only agreed with it but approved it for this presentation. The facts have not changed nor has the recommendation." There was an awkward silence. You could hear the tumbleweed blowing in the wind.

The strategy was approved.

EXAMPLE FIVE

Karen had answered the phone call from a store manager. Karen was hard-working and conscientious in trying to help him with his issues but did not have the authority to grant all of his requests as she was a junior manager. In exasperation he shouted abuse at her and told her, "You have no idea how hard I work. My job would be so much easier if you lazy bastards in the office got off your big, fat arses and helped me!" and then rang off.

Karen was visibly upset and told her boss as she was afraid she would be reported. He contacted the store manager to complain about the abuse of his staff; but the store manager laughed it off and refused to take any action. Karen's boss then wrote an e-mail to the regional manager, copying the store director, insisting that he took disciplinary action or stressing that he would put in an official complaint of his own.

Karen got a full apology from the store manager the next day.

EXAMPLE SIX

Oliver, the MD, had asked for a report on a minor part of the business. Finding himself standing beside Ben, the middle manager he had requested it from, while going into a meeting, he asked when he would see it. Ben replied that he had not forgotten it but it would take another three weeks. "That's just not good enough," said the MD, clearly angry. Ben replied, "Then I think you will have to help me with my priorities. You did not tell me it was urgent." He then listed the four other reports the MD had asked for, all of which were more important and would create greater value, and which Ben had prioritised ahead of this other request.

The priority order remained the same. The minor report was delivered within three weeks. And Oliver never again challenged Ben on the priorities he set for his work-streams.

EXAMPLE SEVEN

It was a major presentation to the board. Bill had spent months working on it and it was a thoroughly well thought-through piece of work. Verne, the MD, asked a penetrating question which had not been addressed. Bill though for a moment and said, "I don't know the answer. We have not researched that. I know how to get that information and I will send it to you by the end of the week."

The decision that Bill wanted on his work was approved pending this last piece of information. Bill duly supplied the data on time, as promised, and it did not contradict the recommendation. The project started on schedule.

EXAMPLE EIGHT

Abby asked her manager to create a report by Friday, in four days' time. Steve looked through his diary, considered his other commitments and thought that it could be achieved. However, by Wednesday, so many issues had turned up that needed addressing immediately, Steve knew he might miss the deadline. Shit happens. Fires needed to be put out.

Steve phoned Abby to explain. "Is there any leeway in the deadline? If not, I am happy to do an all-nighter on Thursday night." Abby replied that her drop-dead date was actually Monday lunchtime as she needed it for the afternoon meeting.

Steve completed the project over the weekend at times that did not inconvenience his young family – the kids' swimming lessons, his partner's bingo night with friends.

First thing on Monday morning he handed over the report to his boss. She tells him to leave early that Friday, and have an early start on the weekend to make up to him for meeting his commitment.

SYNOPSIS OF SECTION FOUR

Personal integrity and the integrity of your leaders is essential. It is the only thing that will give you self-esteem and help to create an "engaged" culture. It's all about trust.

Strangely, integrity will not necessarily make you popular. In a world that frequently seems to be chasing popularity and approval from others, where people-pleasing has become a supreme art to surround yourself with "friends", where superficial timelines and images on social media convince yourself and others of your worth; where "likes" and "friends" have become a target to chase and display – integrity is *not* treasured as valuable. Quite the reverse. Someone with true integrity can make others feel worse about themselves. It is holding up a mirror to their own behaviours, which can be uncomfortable. It can be disconcerting and challenging; it can be confused with arrogance or being difficult.

Having integrity is not an easy way out in life. The easy way is *not* having integrity: just going with the flow, embracing the consensus, flattering the abusive and the powerful, refusing to confront poor intentions or decisions or behaviours. The easy way is following the herd, to ignore your own commitments and not holding authority to account!

And yet all those people who worked with me wanted others with integrity in their lives. And were prepared to hold themselves to behave in that way. What a paradox. **The one value we don't cherish and nurture in ourselves is actually the value we really value most! It is not the people with integrity who are threatening; it is our perception of our own character that comes under threat.** We would all like to think that we are trustworthy and yet it takes little to remind ourselves of when we lacked courage or when we didn't do the right thing because we felt threatened or were under stress or we cheated because no one was looking. Someone is *always* looking – it is us! And our conscience gets pricked when we see someone acting in the way we should have but failed to do.

Why do scandals keep happening? Why is there so much abuse and bullying? Why are Casual Leaders everywhere in our daily lives? It all comes down to this one value. There is simply a lack of real character – a lack of integrity. And we can all try to make that change, starting with ourselves. It's not easy – but nothing worth having ever is. We need to develop our self-awareness, be mindful of others and be clear on what are the right behaviours to live in reasonable harmony with others. We need to be constantly alert to our own intentions and behaviours; we need to practise conscious competence.

After all, WE ARE HOW WE THINK AND WHAT WE BELIEVE IN.

Section five

THE FINAL
WORD

This book is not a text book. It is not an academic study or theory. I set out to write a practical guide to explain the reasons for what really happens in the workplace. I hope to help people who are being used and abused, to encourage them and to suggest ways to change their situations. Perhaps some Casual Leaders might read it and change their ways, for the benefit of all of us and themselves.

Nor is this a book on conventional perceptions of morality. It is usually not a good idea to have a sexual relationship with colleagues and never a good idea to have an extra-marital affair. However, those poor decisions and misjudgements are explicitly a mutual decision between adults; it is the implicit consequences on partners and families that have not been taken into account. And those poor decisions will always have consequences.

No. This is a book about how people treat others within the workplace. It is about how to be the best version of yourself and how to bring out the best in others.

I have tried to expose the one-way street of abuse of power, rank and status. There are real examples of threatening behaviours, intimidation, rudeness, bullying and unfairness. It is never right to deny people respect and rob them of their dignity. Nor to squander the potential of people and create frustration and unhappiness. Some leaders take advantage of others and do not do the job they are paid to do. Too often in the workplace there is callous indifference, laziness and hurtful behaviours from those that are privileged to have been given authority over others. And sometimes these leaders do not even have the self-awareness to understand the consequences of their words and actions.

And, while my own experience is mostly in commercial business, I have deliberately talked about organisations rather than businesses or companies. I believe the observations are universal. I believe they are just as applicable if you are in a school, or a charity, or the civil service, or a voluntary position in an organised activity – or even a political party. This is about basic human psychology and the culture within which we are living today. So this is a story about your rights as an individual within any group setting and how to recognise and establish boundaries of acceptable behaviours.

THE EVIDENCE KEEPS ROLLING IN!

In April 2018, many UK papers reported a survey conducted by SPANA, the international animal charity. The research had interviewed 2,000 employees with alarming results:

o One-third thought they could do a better job than their manager;
o Nearly one-fifth *hated* their manager, had no respect for them, and thought they were the worst thing about their job;
o One in ten thought their boss was "arrogant" or "two-faced";
o More than half of employees surveyed had considered looking for a new job just to get away from their manager.

The research summarised the fifty worst traits of managers, all of which could be addressed:

1 Doesn't communicate well
2 I think they're inconsistent
3 Sets their own rules
4 Doesn't understand my work

5   I think they're incompetent
6   Patronises me
7   Sets a bad example
8   Never says thank you
9   Says one thing and does another
10 Has mood swings
11 I think they're passive–aggressive
12 Brings their personal life to work
13 Obviously favours another member of staff
14 Makes me feel stupid
15 Delegates too much work to me
16 Never gives praise or feedback
17 Doesn't actually do any work
18 Assumes I'm happy to do their work as well as my own
19 I think they're overpaid
20 They think I'm a mind reader
21 I think they're tight with pay rises
22 Sucks up to their own boss
23 Takes credit for other people's work
24 Gives out banter but can't take it
25 Makes me feel guilty for taking time off
26 Doesn't have my back
27 Leaves early every day
28 I think they're tight with bonuses
29 I think they're unqualified for the job
30 Works from home all the time
31 Always picks on one member of staff
32 Has annoying catchphrases
33 Has bad breath
34 Calls me in the evening when I'm not working
35 Listens in to everyone's conversations in the office
36 Repeats the same phrases and jokes over and over again
37 Tells me off in front of everyone instead of in a meeting room

38 Asks for my opinion then claims it as their own
39 Calls me at weekends when I'm not working
40 Makes unfunny jokes
41 Expects everyone to turn up on time when they're always late
42 Awful dress sense
43 Blames me for things they've done wrong
44 Calls me when I'm on holiday
45 Always talks about previous successes
46 Farts
47 I think they're very scruffy
48 Always expects a tea but never/rarely makes one themselves
49 I think they're sexist
50 Bores everyone with their holiday photos and anecdotes

While some are the usual gripes around salary and bonuses, the vast majority are clear evidence of the worst behaviours of Casual Leaders. They are everywhere.

Then, in September 2018, the mental health charity MIND reported a study that showed poor mental health at work was widespread. The research surveyed 44,000 employees, with 48% saying that they had experienced a mental health problem in their current job. Only half of these felt able to talk to their employer, so one in four employees are struggling in silence.

The survey said that critical to a successful outcome is a manager's confidence in knowing how to deal with the issue or even to identify it in the first place. If leaders were able to support and not just concentrate on challenging their employees we would have a much happier workplace. And, while the two studies have not tried to establish a causal link between their findings, I suspect that there must be one, i.e. the behaviours of the Casual Leaders are so prevalent that they cause at least some of the mental health issues within the workplace! So, perhaps, even more critical is that the manager is correctly motivated, accepts a duty of care for their employees and creates an environment that reduces stress, anger, anxiety and frustration.

And in October 2018, the 2017 Skills and Employment Survey of the UK was published. This is a government-funded survey by three top UK universities of 3,300 people and has been running every five years since the 1980s.

The report concluded this year saying that Britons are under more pressure at work than at any time in the last twenty-five years. It found that we are working harder and faster, with increased numbers getting home exhausted. And, despite this, business productivity has stagnated, with UK workers significantly less productive than the average of the G7 countries.

Key findings included that skills were not being trained and that equipment was lacking, while deadlines were becoming more demanding and intense. New technology was being employed to monitor employees and fill their days with tasks while mobile phones and e-mail made it hard for them to switch off out of working hours. The report suggested that autonomy or discretion about how to complete your job had declined sharply from a high of 62% in 1992 to a new low of 38% in 2017 – a clue to increasingly Coercive or Pacesetting leadership styles becoming more prevalent. And it pointed out that reducing individuals' control over their work increased stress and anxiety and led to a higher risk of cardiac illness. Finally, it surveyed zero-hour contract employees for the first time and suggested that the insecurity of employment increased stress and concerns on being victimised or dismissed.

When you review all this evidence, and the rest previously detailed in this book, you will surely conclude that it is imperative that organisations start to address their leadership styles and get rid of the Casual Leaders. They are literally destroying the value of their work by poor behaviours that not only fritter away their employees' potential and reduce their commitment, but also increase health risks.

TEN THINGS YOUR LEADER DESERVES

I have been very critical of certain leaders and of the way organisations behave. And this may help some people to understand what is going on and to make sense of their own situations. To solve a problem, half of the solution is to understand what its root cause is in the first place. But there are some things your leader rightly expects and deserves as well. And I am not sure everyone brings this to their workplace.

1   **Bring the best version of yourself to work every day**
    You are being employed to do a job of work. You must turn up each day bringing the right attitude and energy levels to meet your Work Contract. Time to put on your game-face. And it starts the moment your working day starts – the clock is ticking. I have seen people turn up late to work and then make themselves breakfast, have a good gossip with mates and eventually start their working day an hour after they were paid to start. Or have a leisurely boozy lunch on a Friday and while away the afternoon phoning friends to organise their weekend. Or take two-hour smoking breaks

when they wanted to avoid the next task. It's just not good enough. You are taking money under false pretensions – and that is theft.

Bring the right attitude: be cheerful, enthusiastic, positive, optimistic, helpful, friendly, open-minded and happy to learn. Show curiosity. And be flexible in meeting the demands of the day. Have a can-do attitude.

Bring the right energy: have a good work ethic. Have get-up-and-go energy. Be keen to achieve, purposeful, work with pace, never have idle hands or mind. You are not being paid to gossip or go on your social media accounts or do online shopping. Be determined and persistent in getting the job in hand completed to the best of your ability. Be focussed on the task in hand, be committed, do not waste time or effort, try to be efficient and look for new ways to improve. Be prepared to work.

2 Behave in socially acceptable ways

Role-model the Social Contract. It is all about good teamwork – you will succeed as a team or you will fail as a team – it is rarely about an individual genius.

Be presentable and clean, be inviting, be tolerant, talk straight, laugh politely, be constructive, be inclusive of others, be respectful, disagree politely, support other viewpoints, hear people out, bring empathy, listen actively, give credit to others, compromise, use humour, co-operate, take personal responsibility, offer information and justify your opinions or ideas, accept setbacks.

Be careful with language – never swear at people or call them offensive, derogatory words. Some people find all swearing offensive – I don't because it is the intent behind the words that really matters. It can be a sign of passion, commitment and drive rather than deliberately trying to hurt others. In my book, it is far more offensive not to try your hardest or to shirk the work so your colleagues have to pick up your share too. But no one deserves to be sworn at.

Keep your workstation clean and tidy. Clear up after yourself if using a meeting room – it's not beneath you to show colleagues, cleaners and the facility the respect you want for yourself.

Never interrupt other people's conversations or meetings without a real crisis and a fulsome apology to all. Never answer phone calls, or text, or do e-mails during a meeting or when being presented to. This is more than disrespect; it is downright rude: 0.1% of the time there might be a genuine emergency but 99.9% of the time you are saying, "I am more important than you. Normal rules of behaviour don't apply to me. These people that I am corresponding with are far more important than you!"

Never talk over someone. Always be courteous. *Be an adult.*

3   **Be as competent as you can be**
Understand the organisation and its purpose. Know your role inside out and better than anyone else. Do the work required to the best of your ability. Hone the skills that you have and be honest with the ones you don't. Ask for help. Ask for training, and coaching. Find a mentor. Ask questions and learn as much as you can. Benchmark yourself against the previous person in your job and others at the same level – be determined to perform at a higher level than them and set a new standard. Exceed expectations.

Think like you are the CEO and anticipate the best way to meet the purpose and objectives – don't just sit there waiting to be told what to do.

Ask for more responsibility and show initiative. Don't be happy with being in a comfort zone of a narrow set of skills just to do this job – broaden your knowledge base and develop your skills by asking for new responsibility and new experiences. Develop your ability to solve problems while being aware of all the interests involved plus the repercussions and consequences. Prepare for each and every meeting – do the pre-work and bring the knowledge or input on what is required of you.

4 Work on yourself before criticising others

This is a place of work. You are an adult and need to bring an adult mindset. You must treat your colleagues as adults too.

Are you as aware of yourself as you can be? Do you understand your hot buttons and your reflex reactions to situations and others? Are you in control of your behaviour and your attitudes?

Are you sensitive to others – to their feelings and objectives? Are you as empathetic and as understanding as you can be? Do you support others and are you caring towards them? Are you assertive or just aggressive?

What motivates you? Are you genuinely able to be selfless? Are you co-operative and friendly? Do you want to achieve and be the best you can? Or are you turned on by status, money and power?

5 Be conscientious

Try your hardest. See things through and follow up. Aim for the highest in quality and/or speed – whichever is most appropriate. Look for ways to overcome difficulties or ways to be more efficient. Think through all the possible issues or flaws or barriers. Look for inspiration from other colleagues or other organisations. Everything can be improved and no one has the monopoly on good ideas.

Never break a promise, a commitment or an obligation. If your boss is expecting something from you, make sure you deliver. It is your personal failure if you have forgotten or if you need to be reminded or if you are chased up for it.

Every job has some boring tasks, including some tedious administration. Never shirk it; never cheat on doing it; it's there for a reason. Instead be ruthlessly efficient; boss the admin around by being highly organised and dominate it. Never let it get it out of hand and become the job either.

6   Have good intent

Examine what is motivating you. Are you giving goodwill to all your colleagues? Are you behaving with respect? Are you trying your hardest to support others and to be a good citizen? This is all about the team – are you being a good team player?

Own up to mistakes or problems. Do not bullshit or lie; do not cover it up or hope no one finds out. Be honest and responsible at all times in the interests of your colleagues and the organisation.

Never break the law! And this includes all internal rules for the organisation such as expenses.

Never endanger yourself or others, either physically, emotionally or psychologically.

7   Always be on time

Being on time is all about respect. Others have put aside their time for you. They have all got other things to be doing, other demands on their time. If you turn up late you are being disrespectful; it does not matter if it is one colleague or a whole meeting of them. It does not matter if they are people who report into you, or if you work alongside them or they have higher status than you. It does not matter if they are suppliers or contractors or guests. It does not matter if they are visitors or you are interviewing a candidate for a job. If you turn up late to anyone, you are saying, "You don't matter. I could not be bothered to be organised. I am more important than you."

Being late is just disrespectful. If you turn up five minutes early, you are on time. If you turn up on time, you are late. If you turn up five minutes late you should be censured!

There will always be reasons for lateness beyond your control – delayed trains, traffic issues, immediate crises, etc. – SH*T HAPPENS! In these circumstances always anticipate lateness and contact your host to advise them before you are actually late. Give a responsible estimate of how long you will be late – and apologise to everyone when you get there. This is not just good manners – this is all about having the humility to show respect.

8 Communicate effectively

Communication is a skill to be learnt. How to be precise and accurate, how to be concise and to the point. But you also need to be appropriate in your method of communication and your timing.

E-mail should be seen as a last resort. Can you say it in person? Can you phone and talk directly? And when writing an e-mail, construct it as a personal note or a letter. Do not see it as an excuse to be curt and dispense with common civility. Do not use it is as a broadcasting tool such as a radio programme or an announcer speaker system. Too many people clog the airwaves by trying to show how clever they are or how hard they have worked. As a result around 80% of my inbox was full of rubbish. It was either stuff I did not need to know or messages where I was not being asked for or being given information. Once I got an e-mail chain of sixteen messages. I was being copied into every exchange between two junior managers as they tried to meet up together – I could not care less that they were meeting or how incompatible their diaries were. Time for some common sense as I was getting 150 e-mails a day but only needed about twenty-five of them.

And blind-copy e-mails – where correspondents are secretly seeing the e-mails – are just wrong. This is dishonest, cowardly and furtive in my opinion. If you don't want people to know who is seeing the correspondence, you are treating them as either untrustworthy or as a conspirator and a spy. If you cannot be open and honest in your correspondence, you should not be saying it at all.

However, you must also be timely in any communication. Your leader should never find out anything substantial without prior knowledge from you. Do not surprise them; manage expectations and let them know of progress, issues, delays or implications before it is too late. And don't abuse their Work Contract by sending e-mails late at night or at weekends or when they are on holiday. Just as you have a Work Contract, so does your boss.

9 Have integrity

This is so important, it had an earlier chapter all on its own. Remember, if you want people to have integrity in their dealings with you – and everyone does – then you *must* reciprocate and have integrity in dealing with them. It is a two-way street and you have as much responsibility as anyone else.

Integrity creates trust. Show you are worthy of being trusted.

10 And finally... give your boss the benefit of the doubt!

They are human too. They will make mistakes. They will be less sensitive than they should be at times. They have full in-trays and multiple demands on them just as you have. They are not devoting 100% of their day to just worrying about you.

No one has all the answers. No one is perfect. And some bosses may still be learning the ropes of management. They will not get everything right, first time and with everyone. I have made loads of mistakes in my career and I am sure some people are reading this book with raised eyebrows that I am the author. However, I would like to think I started out with good intent, tried my hardest and got better as a leader as my experience grew.

So give your leader the benefit of the doubt and be adult enough to raise concerns with them – rather than sitting back and grumbling with colleagues. Choose a private space where no one is self-conscious and there are no prying ears. Talk to them as an adult and expect an adult reply. You might be surprised by the result. Perhaps they just did not know there was an issue in the first place.

If you do all the things above you are starting to role-model the leader you deserve. You don't need people reporting into you to be a leader; you need the mindset of one. You can inspire others. Show people the best way to behave and let's start the revolution upwards!

FIVE THINGS LEADERS CANNOT DEMAND

1 **Every waking hour**

You have a Work Contract. Only Casual Leaders try to ignore this and make excessive demands on you. In reality, they have no power to enforce anything over and above that contract and are trading on your fear of consequences when they demand more.

We all have a responsibility to be flexible and compliant to the needs of the job. But it is when this is taken for granted and demanded all the time that the Casual Leader is at fault. They are being the bullies in the playground and you know from experience how that ends if you try to appease them. Remind them of your rights and the boundaries that are in your contract.

2 **Your self-respect and your dignity**

You never said that this was something you would sacrifice. Don't! These are fundamentals of the Social Contract that each and every one of us share.

Never allow yourself to be shouted at, to be humiliated, to be ridiculed, to be embarrassed, to be belittled, or to be brow-beaten.

Never accept abuse, or bullying or harassment. No one has the right to be dismissive of you or to show contempt.

At the end of the day, we teach people how to treat us. If you allow this behaviour once, you will get it time and time again. Better to stop it from the outset, and suffer a temporary confrontation, than allow the toxic effects to erode your confidence and how you feel about yourself.

Remember, outside of work you are an independent, autonomous adult. That is a powerful place and society holds you to account for your actions. That does not change because you are in a place of work. If you want to be treated as a powerful adult, behave like one, and refuse to be treated as a powerless child.

3 Your reputation

Your reputation is yours and yours alone. Your happiness at work now, and your prospects for the future, rest entirely on your reputation.

Make sure that perceptions of you are honest and accurate always. And the best way to do this is by having integrity at the core of all your actions, behaviours and attitude. If this is unshakeable then no amount of misinformation will stick to your reputation.

4 Your health or your safety

We all take these things for granted and take foolish risks. That is human nature and experts say men are worse than women for doing so. It is only when we lose our health or become endangered that we realise the risks that we have taken and regret it. At least these were the consequences of our own actions.

But your leader cannot demand that you risk your health or your safety against your wishes. They have no right to endanger you or your ability to derive a livelihood – so don't let them! And this means your emotional and your psychological health too.

5   **Your personal loyalty**
You may find that your leader expects a level of personal loyalty from you. They may even demand it or punish you for any perceived lack of it. This is just blackmail or coercion.

Your personal loyalty is yours to give. Do not confuse your line manager with a friend. They have a job to do and they have responsibility over you – that is not a friendship. That is not a mutual exchange between two equals on a level playing field. You can have both a thoroughly harmonious and professional relationship with each other without trying to extort an emotional allegiance – so it's best if it is kept that way, for both of you. Loyalty, like trust, has to be earned!

If you find yourself having any of these five things being demanded of you... if you are being led by a Casual Leader... if you have tried every opportunity to change the situation... if no other recourse is available to you – support from colleagues, the management line, HR department, internal grievances procedures – if your leader is just unreasonable, i.e. cannot be reasoned with... if the leader in question has so much power that no one will assist you... THEN GET OUT!

Life is too short to be unhappy. You will spend anything up to one-third of your time in any given working week at your organisation. It should be fulfilling and give you satisfaction. And if your Casual Leader prevents that in your current organisation, just go to an organisation that can. It's just not worth it to put up and shut up. And there are plenty of good leaders and "engaged" cultures out there – go find one because YOU DESERVE IT.

THANK YOU!

I could be thanking you for reading this book. And I am grateful if you waded through it or even just paid for it. And I do hope that someone, somewhere has found my ramblings useful and it has inspired them to take action.

But my real thank you is to those real leaders that I came across in my career. To those people who set me an example of what it is to really be a leader. That showed me that leadership is all about strength of character and particularly integrity and humility.

What I learnt was that leadership is not a training course; it is not a tick-box exercise; it is not just a set of rules and procedures to be learnt and followed. It is something that comes from deep down inside of an individual. It is a testimony to the core of an individual's sense of identity and decency.

And any one of us can be a leader. You don't need to be in charge of other people and hold a management position. Each of us can take responsibility for how we think, feel and act towards others. We can all be leaders in this way and become a positive part of society – both at work and in the wider world.

Unfairly, I singled out just four individuals in my opening chapter – my heroes of good leadership. And, while examples are sparse, the lack of leaders out there is probably nowhere near as limited as just four people in a thirty-five-year career!

I could easily have mentioned: Nick Varney, Howard Southern, David Rowlands, Sue Walsh, Darroch Bagshaw, Jay Gadialli, Alan Ransome, David Allard, Louise Wardle, Paul Hudson, Mark Rapley, Caroline Jackson, Marc McGuigan, John Owen, Chris Smith, Ned Buck, David Brewis, Gary Moss, Brian Hannon, Bridget Renwick, Jonathan Webster, Jonathan Lawson, Steve Magnall, Steve Jebson, Paul Willcock, Peter Groves, Gary Cowles, Jean Bouvain, Simon Ponsonby, John Weir or Andrew Christophers. And so many others who I feel sure were good leaders on the evidence that I saw.

I chose the four leaders to highlight carefully. I don't just feel sure that they were good leaders – I can guarantee it! I worked for or alongside these four individuals for many years. I saw their behaviours under countless challenges and difficult circumstances. I know that many of them had to stand up to Casual Leaders in their own careers and risk consequences for doing so. And I feel absolutely certain that they met the criteria I have laid out in this book: adults, well motivated with good intent, good self-awareness, high emotional and social intelligence, respect for the Social and Work Contracts etc. But, most importantly of all, these four people stood out for their decency, for their strength of character, and they were shining examples of integrity and humility.

So I would like to thank: Bernard Bremer, Roz Boulstridge, Bob Jones and Tim May. My life and my career have been immeasurably better for knowing you. You set me a fantastic example to live up to and encouraged me to be a better version of myself. In a world that is often shallow and selfish, you have stood out for decency and hard work. You know that people have a responsibility to do more and that leadership is not an excuse to do less. So I am enormously and sincerely grateful to have met you and shared so many experiences with you. Thank you; it has been a pleasure to have known you.